The Glory Walk

The Glory Walk

Living on Purpose for the Glory of God

JAMES R. WILKES

RESOURCE *Publications* · Eugene, Oregon

THE GLORY WALK
Living on Purpose for the Glory of God

Resource Publications
An Imprint of Wipf and Stock Publishers
199 W. 8th Ave., Suite 3
Eugene, OR 97401
www.wipfandstock.com

ISBN 13: 978-1-60899-356-7

Manufactured in the U.S.A.

*Dedicated to my beloved wife and best friend, Mary,
who runs along side of me in this grace race*

Contents

Preface

ONE WEEK in the summer of 2009, in a quaint cottage by the Atlantic Ocean in southern Maine, I typed away on my laptop completing this book. My wife was with me and patiently occupied her time while I busily wrote away. I had something on my heart. I still do—my purpose here on earth. I did not always know that I existed to glorify God and enjoy him. Most of my early years were spent exalting in myself! God is merciful and gracious. His amazing grace saved a wretch like me through Jesus Christ. Even then, it took me a long time to realize some of the very things I write about in these pages. Putting them into practice is even harder. There is so much of my old thinking and behavior yet to be put to death in practice. It will take a miracle—I am glad that I have the promise that it will happen by God's future grace!

It is my understanding that Johann Sebastian Bach used to write the letters S.D.G. at the bottom of each one of his musical compositions. This was to let everyone know that God alone was to be glorified in Bach's works. You see S.D.G. stood for the Latin words *Soli Deo Gloria* (Glory to God alone). I certainly do not think that this book is the work of art that Bach's compositions are! But if it helps you to understand your purpose in life better . . .

S.D.G.

1

Seeing the Big Picture of God's Kingdom

I HAVE a tendency to live in my own little world. I don't mean that I never watch the news or keep up with what is going on in the world. With all the various media sources, I manage to keep informed at least to some extent. What I do mean is that my natural tendency is not to see the bigger picture that I have been made a part of in Jesus Christ. I can get so busy with the ordinary duties of life that my vision of what is real and important sometimes gets blurred. Life can become a daily grind so to speak. Life can become all about my circumstances, my struggles, my relationships, my duties—all beginning with me and ending with me. But there is much more going on. As a Christian, I must see it. I must be involved in it. It is important for me to be aware of what is really going on, participate properly, and be alive to the real world of God's kingdom. My need is that I see this bigger picture and live in the light of it. I have called it a *bigger picture* but it is really the biggest picture. It is what is real, what is most valuable, and what is most important. Most Christians need some help seeing this big picture. This is the reason for this book. This big picture is what all believers desperately need to be aware of and live in the light of. We must come out of our own little self-focused world and see more clearly what God has done and is doing through Jesus Christ. So I am going to begin with a basic explanation of just what this big picture is that Christians need to see. Let me start my explanation, not by going back to the beginning of creation, but by going back to a believer's actual entrance in time to the kingdom of Christ. Colossians 1:13 speaks of this event in this way: "He has delivered us from the power of darkness and conveyed *us* into the kingdom of the Son of His love." At conversion to Christ, believers are taken from the realm of darkness and placed into the kingdom of Christ. From that point on, life must never be the same. Let me point out three important elements of this realm that we have been brought into in Christ. Then let me point out their significance.

THE BIG PICTURE: GOD'S GLORY

First, let us consider God's aim in saving us. It is clear that he saved us by the gospel (good news). It is not by any works that we have done. We were saved by grace alone through faith alone (Ephesians 2:8–9). In 1 Corinthians chapter 1, Paul is speaking of the power of the cross for those who believe. He points out that to the world of Jews and Gentiles the cross is a stumbling block and foolishness (v.23). God saves people through that which the unregenerate heart perceives as foolish. He demonstrates his wisdom by confounding the foolish pride of men (v.27). He saves men through the cross. In the cross, God shows human beings that they are weak not strong, wicked not good, rebellious not submissive. He does all the work of redemption because he is merciful and lovingly kind. The chapter comes to a climax by pointing to

God's great aim, "that no flesh should glory in His presence" (v.29). It is emphatically stated again in verse 31: "He who glories let him glory in the LORD." God is to be glorified because men are simply sinful creatures. God is to be glorified because men are entirely dependent on God to save them. Thus it is God's great aim in salvation to be known for his glory. He must be exalted. His name must be magnified. He is worthy to receive all of the believer's praise and honor. This is what our new world is about. The kingdom we have been placed into is a kingdom where God's glory is supreme. That is the first key element in our picture—God alone is to be glorified. This first element is the primary one and will be the focus of this book. However, the other two elements are important to see as well.

THE BIG PICTURE: CHRIST IS LORD

The second element I want to point out about a believer's new realm is that it is a realm of lordship. It has a king. It has someone who rules over it with love, kindness, goodness, justice, and grace. The king is all-powerful and all-wise. My point is basically that which we have already seen in Colossians 1:13. Believers have been conveyed into "the kingdom of the Son." He does not merely rule because he is God. He rules because he has conquered sin, hell, and death on the cross. Jesus Christ has satisfied the wrath of God the Father by bearing it himself. Christ's triumph on the cross was certified in his resurrection on the third day. He rose from the grave with new life, the new life that he gives to all who believe on him. So the kingdom we have been brought into is ruled by a king who is glorious. He is the reason we are saved. All our boasting is to be in him. He is truly Lord. He is a most worthy king, having bought the salvation of all of his subjects with his own blood. He is a gracious king, saving his people from the realm of eternal darkness. So in our new kingdom, God alone is to be glorified, and Jesus Christ is to be our Lord. Now for the last element.

THE BIG PICTURE: WE SEE GOD'S GREATNESS

The third element of this kingdom is that believers now have their eyes opened that they may see the glorious character of their king. Paul puts it this way in 2 Corinthians 4:6: "For it is the God who commanded light to shine out of darkness, who has shone in our hearts to *give* the light of the knowledge of the glory of God in the face of Jesus Christ." When we are placed into his kingdom, we have the privilege to see his glory, especially in our salvation. We begin to see how great our God truly is. God opens up our eyes progressively to his greatness. We begin to see the perfection and beauty of his character. The Psalmist's words in Psalm 145:8–10 come alive to our hearts: "The LORD *is* gracious and full of compassion, Slow to anger and great in mercy. The LORD *is* good to all, And His tender mercies *are* over all His works. All Your works shall praise You, O LORD, And Your saints shall bless You." Christ's kingdom is about his glory, his Lordship, and his excellence. What a spectacular realm we have been brought into by God's grace! What is to be our response?

Certainly an event like our translation into Christ's kingdom must be seen as life-changing. It is not just one of many important events in one's life; it is *the* important event of one's life. The alternative is eternal darkness. The alternative is torment so awful as to be presently incomprehensible. We have been delivered from this negative realm and the eternal consequences that we deserved. We have been brought into this glorious realm which has at its center God himself! We will ultimately be brought into eternal joy forever. Let me now briefly offer responses to the three elements discussed above.

HUMILITY, OBEDIENCE, WORSHIP, AND JOY

God's saving us by the cross for his glory must surely humble us. If we now walk in the light of the bigger picture, we will walk this earth humbly before God. We will recognize our dependence completely upon him. The gospel is God doing for us what we could not do for ourselves. It is good news for us. God does the doing. We do the receiving. God is the giver. We are the getters. We get his grace and mercy. We are indwelt by his Spirit. We have his power working in and through us. There is no room for our boasting at all (Romans 3:27; Galatians 6:14). We have been made a part of God's assembly of saints. It happened because of his work. This does not mean that our pilgrim walk in this world will be easy. Though we have entered a new realm, it has not been fully realized yet. Bad things will still happen. There is still struggle and pain. There are still battles to be won. There is still work to be done. My point is that as we live out the Christian life, we must live in light of our new position in our new realm. We must understand that in everything that happens, God must be known for his glory. We must walk humbly. We must exalt him. This book has been written to help you to see the bigger picture and humbly glorify God on purpose.

Since Christ is the Lord of this new realm, our response must be simple obedience. That is the mark of one who has been brought into the kingdom. Jesus explained it like this: "If you abide in My word, you are My disciples indeed" (John 8:31). You see there were a lot of people around Christ while He ministered on earth that had a very spurious faith. They were curious and wanted to see miracles. But their faith had no real substance. Those who are truly in the kingdom, recognize Christ's Lordship and desire to obey. I am not saying that believers are perfect. Far from it! I am saying that there is a desire to follow Christ from the heart that shows up in real life. The more we see ourselves in the big picture, the more we will humbly follow the one who is our King. So in response to God's glory in the cross, we ought to be humbly dependant. In response to His Lordship, we should be obedient followers. This book has been written to help you glorify God as a humble follower.

Let's now consider our response to God's character. It requires worship. When we see God as he truly is, we must bow our hearts and proclaim his worth. Since the Lord is so great in his character, he is to be greatly praised (Psalm 96:4). When we walk in the reality of God's kingdom, our hearts will be praising God all the time. But there is more. God's character brings forth joy. Our praise is willing. God is a delight to our souls. His character is so pleasing. God's kingdom is not characterized by unfeeling duty. It is characterized by blessed delight. We joy in the God of our salvation. In fact, so great is this joy, so real is this response to be, that Paul tells us to "Rejoice in the Lord always" (Philippians

4:4). Imagine that kind of joy! Paul is calling for an abiding joy, one that never lets up. So, in this new realm, we see that God has saved us so that he gets all of the glory. Thus, we are to walk humbly in dependence upon him. Christ is the supreme Lord. Thus, we follow him in simple obedience. God's great character shines brightly forth. Thus, we worship and rejoice.

I believe that for these responses to be present in our daily lives, this bigger picture must be in our view continually. We all have that tendency to walk in our own little world. We tend to see ourselves as the beginning and end of every event. We must learn to walk in Christ's kingdom. We must see that it is not simply about us. We must see that there is something much, much bigger and better! We must live to glorify our King. My prayer for you then is that this book will be used by God to help you grow in God's glorious purposes. The pull to be man-centered is great. The pull to be self-focused is real. But God's grace is sufficient. The struggles we face at times are fierce. But God's victory is assured. It certainly helps to know God's aim in saving us. This book has been written to be a help in making the goal clear—we must glorify God alone. We must see all that comes our way in the light of his kingdom. Every event of our lives must be God-focused. When we are sick, something even more important is going on. We must see it and glorify God in our sickness. When we are struggling financially, we must see that something more important is going on. We must see it and glorify God in our financial struggles. When we go to church, we must see the bigger picture and worship, fellowship, learn, and grow. Do you see the point? We are members of Christ's kingdom. This calls for a radically different kind of living. Our lives are a part of something vastly greater than ourselves. It is wonderful, yet it is radical. We must live drastically different from the world. We must approach living for God's glory with the seriousness it deserves. So let's explore what it means to live in the light of the bigger picture of God's kingdom. Let's see what it means to be concerned about glorifying God alone. Let's look at this glory walk.

2

Five Huge Truths

Gᴏᴅ's ɢʟᴏʀʏ—ᴡʜᴀᴛ does that mean to you? As a Christian, it should mean a great deal. Actually it needs to be central to every part of your life! The leaders of the first epoch of the Protestant Reformation affirmed what are known as the five *sola's*—*sola fide* (faith alone*), sola Scriptura* (Scripture alone), *solus Christus* (Christ alone), *sola gratia* (grace alone) and *soli Deo Gloria* (God's glory alone). The one I want to emphasize here is *soli Deo Gloria*. These reformers all agreed that believers in Jesus Christ should live for God's glory exclusively. The Westminster Catechism puts it like this: "Man's chief end is to glorify God and enjoy him forever." Two important verses that address this are Isaiah 43:7 and 1 Corinthians 10:31. Isaiah 43:7 specifically tells us that God created us for his glory. The apostle Paul reinforces this when he writes in I Corinthians 10:31 that believers should do everything they do to the glory of God. God's glory is actually at the heart of the Bible. Throughout the pages of Scripture, God reveals himself as the Supreme Being to whom belongs all glory. However, since we live in a world that has been corrupted by sin, man is constantly trying to take center-stage. Even the contemporary church seems to be held captive to man-centeredness. It must not be so among genuine believers. Those God has saved by his grace must recognize the glory of God and live intentionally to make much of him. The purpose of this book is to help believers understand God's glory more fully so that they then may live with the purpose of continually glorifying him. Our focus must be Godward. It is so easy for contemporary believers in Jesus Christ to get off track in this area. There is so much man-centeredness—so many temptations to exalt oneself. I believe many in the professing church are profoundly man-centered. Many professing evangelical Christians have never really been on the right track when it comes to glorifying God. We must face the reality that our culture is man-centered, our natural tendency is toward self-glory, and we desperately need the grace of God to fulfill our purpose in God's created order! I am saying that we must live for God's glory by his amazing grace.

I am not writing this book from the perspective of a casual observer. I write with a very burdened heart. I write as someone who has served for many years in ministry with a skewed focus. Although I paid lip service to God, his glory was not truly my central focus. I have been a Christian for some thirty-one years. I came to Christ in my late twenties. God graciously saved me from the depths of unbelief. Yet, for much of my own Christian life, there were so many things that were supposed to be spiritual that actually got in the way of living for God's glory. Although much of my Christian life has been spent in ministry, it has not been spent actually understanding the great truths concerning God's glory or his grace in salvation. I praise God for his merciful deliverance from an overly man-centered way of living the Christian life. Thus, this chapter is about some of the great truths God has revealed to us that lead us away from man-centeredness. So before we begin an actual discussion on what God's glory means (chapter 3) or what it means for us to live for his glory (chapter 4), I want to begin with five huge, amazing, significant truths that point us in the right direction. These truths are *big picture* truths that are of vital importance as we live in the new realm of Christ's kingdom. These truths might even be contrary to what you have come to believe as a Christian. Yet, they are foundational truths that have enormous implications. These truths have helped me, by God's grace, to become more God-centered. So I want to encourage you to prayerfully consider these truths. When really grasped, they are life-changing. Ask God to really open up your heart that you may have a deep understanding of these wonderful principles of Scripture. I find that many believers do not take the time needed to let these truths actually sink in. There is not a lot of reflection on the deep things of God. People are too busy. Believers are too busy. But these truths are worthy of deep reflection. They need to be genuinely understood. So take your time reading this foundational chapter. Stop and reflect on the verses and their underlying meaning. Look up the verses referenced. These truths will help us along the way as we seek to see the importance of God being at the center of our lives. The truths presented here will undergird the rest of the discussion in this book. I need to mention one final preliminary thought. My desire is to be biblical. At the end of the day it does not matter what you think or what I think. It matters what God thinks! With these things in mind, let's look at these five huge truths.

YOU DO NOT DESERVE TO BE SAVED

Now, I can already see some readers nodding their heads and saying "I already know that!" But do not let go of this truth so quickly. I believe that Christians must grow in their sense of lostness. It is important to understand the degree of our undeservedness. None of us is worthy, deserving, of great value, special, or loveable from God's perspective. The nature that we are born with is naturally bad and not at all good. I know this is not pleasant. I know in our self-esteem saturated culture this does not go over well. It is, however, the biblical teaching. My wife actually has some acquaintances that cannot tolerate it whenever she makes a comment about her not deserving something. They are so steeped in the idea of self-worth that they tell her they cannot stand it when she says it. They tell her that she is deserving of good things. This is the normal thinking of our culture. We must make much of ourselves. It is only right for we are certainly worthy. The truth God has revealed to us is quite different. None of us deserve anything good. Every good part of our lives is a gift of God's grace. We deserve only condemnation, and certainly we do not deserve to be saved from our sinful, rebellious condition! When it comes to our position under God, we actually have no rights whatsoever. This is not some wild, extreme, cult-ish teaching. It is actually a basic truth in Scripture that is just plain orthodox. We are sinners by nature. We are unde-serving. Saying we are saved by grace is not something that Christians should just give lip-service to. It should be a pro-found reality that we understand, believe, and let affect our hearts. We human beings are rebels against the living and true God. This makes the fact that God saved us so glorious. It adds to our understanding of his worthiness of all praise. We must have a proper understanding of our sinfulness to truly appreciate God's glory and grace. Not long ago I actually preached a message in which I stated that focusing on one's sinfulness was not necessarily a bad thing! We must see the truth about who we are as fallen human beings. This does not always set well as it falls on modern man's ears. Thinking that we are something great is an idea that has to fall, if we will truly glorify God. After conversion to Christ, it is still important that we continually see what God has done and is doing for sinners such as us. Do you see how this helps us stay focused on God and helps us give him the glory? Our sinfulness ought to force us to look upward. Our spiritual poverty should compel us to look to God. So contemplate your natural sinfulness and rebellion all you want. Only be sure that your contemplation leads you to the cross of Christ not to despair.

So let's briefly look at the biblical picture. After the fall of man, the Scripture points out the fact that all men are in rebellion against God. Romans 8:7–8 states, "Because the carnal mind *is* enmity against God; for it is not subject to the law of God, nor indeed can be. So then, those who are in the flesh cannot please God." This means that the unconverted mind is hostile toward God. The unsaved person cannot do anything that pleases God. Theologians speak of the doctrine of total depravity. The *total* does not mean that every person is as wicked as can be. Sinful people can behave kindly, do good deeds, and love their children. Even the worst criminals in the history of the world more than likely were kind to someone along the way. Human beings are not void of qualities pleasing to man and beneficial to society when viewed strictly on a human level. People build hospitals and feed the hungry. Even in Massachusetts, where I live, every once in a while a driver will stop at a busy intersection and let you go! What total depravity actually means is that sin affects every part of our being—our intellect, heart, will—the whole works. Romans 3:10–18 speaks to this point. In these verses, we can see the universality of sin (its extensiveness) and the depth of sin (its intensiveness). Sin corrupts our understanding. No one seeks after God. No one is righteous. No one really wants to worship and respect God. The passage ends with these words: "There is no fear of God before their eyes (v.18)."

Before we leave this subject, let me point out two more important truths. First of all, sin is not simply violating a list of prohibitions. Sin is against God. We must see the weight of our human sinfulness. We have offended God—the absolute, holy, sovereign, only true God. God offers himself as the supreme treasure that he is, and we reject him. This is the ultimate height of our sinfulness. It is not taking cookies from the cookie jar when told not to. It is not lying on a tax return. These things are certainly wrong. However, the worst aspect of our sinfulness is that we do not honor God as we should. We do not love him with all of our intellect, emotions, and strength. Jesus said that this was the greatest commandment (Matthew 22:37). We do not stand in awe of God as we should. We do not recognize his worthiness. We do not worship him properly. All of our sin flows out of this inner rebellion we have toward God. Secondly, our sinful nature renders us unwilling and unable to respond to God in any positive way. I am not saying that sinful men cannot respond to God. Sinful people are constantly responding to God but in rebellion. However, sinful men do not respond to God in love and in seeking to glorify him.

There is so much more that God has revealed on this subject. Here are some other scriptural thoughts you might want to reflect on: man's spiritual deadness (Ephesians 2:1–3); the deceitful wickedness of man's heart (Jeremiah 17:9); that the heart of man is the real problem (Mark 7:21–23); that everyone truly falls short of giving God proper glory (Romans 3:23); that unregenerate men do not welcome and cannot understand spiritual truth (I Corinthians 2:14). We do not deserve to be saved. Yet, I encounter many who profess to know Christ, who seem to think that God owes them something. In fact, I would suggest that by and large human beings think that God owes a lot to them. I hear many times about believers who are angry at God! You can be sure that when someone is angry at God, they do not understand truly who God is and who they are. Many times, when bad things happen, we seem to think that we are in a position to judge God, to give him a thumbs-down on how he is ruling the world or our lives. Perhaps, if we feel really gracious, we will excuse him, for the moment. We will give him a second chance. All this is foolishness. The truth that we do not deserve to be saved (and, in fact, do deserve eternal punishment) is so important to understand. It makes grace what it truly is—undeserved favor. We must be amazed at God's grace, love, and mercy. We were spiritually blind and God gave us sight (Ephesians 4:18). We were spiritually deaf and God gave us hearing (John 8:43). We would not come to him, but he graciously drew us (John 6:44). We were spiritually dead and he made us alive (Ephesians 2:5).

We must not simply say that God's grace is amazing. We must actually be amazed. We must not simply say that God should be glorified in all things; we must truly recognize his worthiness. What a huge truth! You and I do not deserve to be saved!

GOD HAS NO NEEDS

Every believer does theology. Some just do it very poorly. You see, essentially, theology is simply what one thinks about God. Far too often our thoughts about God consist of our own ideas. One great need in contemporary evangelicalism is that we seek to know God as he has revealed himself to us in his word. In other words, believers need to do theology well! The following is a theological understanding of God that surely is filled with faulty thinking. I have heard statements like this hypothetical one:

> In the beginning, God was lonely. He needed to create some people to make him complete. He needed some people to love and to fellowship with. So he made man. When men fell into sin, God came up with a plan to redeem them. He sent his Son to pay for their sins and now he is trying to bring these people to himself, because he needs their fellowship. He also needs the help of all of those who have come to know him. He needs them to work for him. If they don't do the job, it will all be in vain. How wonderful we can feel, knowing that we are helping God. We feel good when we lend our neighbors a hand. How much more so, when we help God out!

Not all in the above statement is completely wrong. Just wrong enough to make a big difference as to whether or not you glorify God with your life. Our second huge truth is that God has no needs. He did not create human beings from his need to have fellowship. He was not lonely. He is not dependent on us in any way. It is quite the opposite. We are completely dependent on him. The more we realize our dependence on God, the more he is actually glorified! Let's briefly examine this Biblically. God is completely self-sufficient. As theologian Bruce Ware puts it:

> Not only is God's transcendence displayed in his utter distinction from all lesser contingent reality and in his eternal self-existence, but the transcendence of God finds full expression in the conception of God's absolute self-sufficiency. God exists eternally by his own will and nature, and his existence is of such a quality as to contain intrinsically every quality in infinite measure. The eternal existence of God is the eternal existence of all perfection, infinitely and intrinsically possessed, within the eternal triune nature of God. Just as it is unthinkable from a biblical point of view that God could ever not be, so too it is unimaginable that God could ever receive some quality, some value, some knowledge, some power, some ability, some perfection that he previously lacked.[1]

God does not owe his existence to anyone or anything else. He has life in himself. He is self-existent and independent (John 5:26). In his independence, God has no needs.

1. Ware, *God's Greater Glory*, 48.

Acts 17:25 states, "Nor is he worshiped with men's hands, as though he needed anything, since he gives to all life, breath, and all things." here it is clear that God is the source of everything and that he himself needs nothing. The word *worshiped* is *therapeuo*. It has the idea of taking care of someone, healing someone, serving someone. In this verse, Paul is stating that no one takes care of God or ministers to his needs! In this sense, no one serves God nor can they serve God. When we speak of glorifying God, we must be clear that it does not mean that we add anything at all to God. We do not make him greater or more glorious. He is infinitely great and glorious no matter what we do or do not do. No one controls God. He controls all things. He has ordained all things and he will providentially accomplish all of his good and perfect will (Psalm 115:3; Ephesians 1:11). God is, by his nature, Lord over all. All creatures are, by necessity, dependent on this independent God! He is truly the "High and Lofty One that inhabits eternity whose name is holy . . ." (Isaiah 57:15).

God's transcendence above his creation means that his creation must stand in awe of him. Psalm 33:8 says, "Let all the earth fear the LORD; Let all the inhabitants of the world stand in awe of him." We will not understand God completely because of his infinite greatness (Psalm 145:3). God is supremely above us and is perfect. Everything he does is perfect. He makes no mistakes. He never sins. Questioning God's character and judgments must be seen as foolish. God does not own up to a standard outside of himself. His ways are perfect and consistent with his goodness of character. He is beyond reproach (Deuteronomy 32:4). We must worship him alone for he alone is the living and true God.

In all of what I have written above, my ultimate point is this: when this transcendent God pays attention to us (and he does—big time through Jesus Christ), we should deem him as worthy not ourselves. He created humankind so that we could know him and experience the greatness of his being. We were created in his image so that we could reflect his glory. In other words—it is all about him! Our fullest joy, satisfaction and pleasure comes from experiencing this transcendent God (Psalm 16:11).

THE GOSPEL IS FOR YOUR ENTIRE LIFE

Recently I heard a preacher speaking of his ministry. In essence, he said that his ministry was to give the gospel to the lost. Then after people embrace the gospel, he teaches them so that they may serve God. One might summarize this as the win them, work them concept of ministry. In my experience, this is quite common. We enter the kingdom humbly through the cross. Then, we move on to serve God and gain his favor by our own self-efforts. This is absolutely disastrous. The idea of embracing the gospel and then moving on has a devastating effect on a believer's life. We must never move away from the gospel. We must only grow deeper in the gospel. Let me explain why this is true and so important. First of all, our relationship with God is gospel-dependent. We never relate to him based upon what we do—only based upon what Christ has done. We must remember that the gospel is good news not good advice. It is the news that Jesus Christ came into the world to save sinners like us. He lived in perfect obedience to his Father's will. He died on the cross as a substitute for sinners. Those who believe on him have his righteousness counted on their behalf. They have their sins forgiven. They are given eternal life. This is all by God's grace. There is no merit whatsoever on the part of the sinner. I recently heard someone illustrate the difference between good news and good advice. Good advice is when a teacher prepares her fifth grade class for the big history exam by telling them what to study. During the exam, she sees one student who looks hopelessly lost. She stands beside his desk and encourages him by telling him to relax and try his best to remember what he has learned—still just good advice. He is however still hopelessly lost. Now, good news is if she says to him, "Scoot over." She then sits beside him and takes the test for him. Good news indeed! He goes from hopeless failure to sure success. That is the gospel. In the gospel, God does something for you that you could never do for yourself. He saves you eternally. Thus, you must realize that when you come before God, you only come before him because of the gospel, because of what he has done, because of his grace. Those who think they are done with the gospel once they are saved, begin to perform for God rather than depend on God. The danger of slipping into a self-righteous mindset is extremely great.

Also, when we cling to the cross of Christ, we continue to feel and experience his grace. We are kept from slipping into despair, because we realize all that he has done for us and continues to do. We recognize that we are continual recipients of grace. This is the very opposite of seeking to merit his favor. That is why it is important to grow in gospel truths; to understand, more and more, all the spiritual blessings that are attached to the gospel of Jesus Christ. When we realize the hope that comes with the gospel (Ephesians

1:18), the sufficiency of Christ's grace (2 Corinthians 12:9), the access we have to God's throne (Hebrews 4:16), and so much more, we are greatly encouraged to be steadfast in our walk with God.

It is, in addition, a great truth that it is from our position in Christ that we successfully engage in spiritual battle. When one moves away from the cross (the gospel) one moves away from the very position that assures victory. Consider, very briefly, the great gospel words of Romans 6:11, "Likewise you also, reckon yourselves to be dead indeed to sin, but alive to God in Christ Jesus our Lord." The word *reckon* here means *to regard as*. How can one regard himself to be dead to sin unless that is a reality of the gospel? How can one regard himself as alive to God unless that is also a reality of the gospel? God is not playing a cruel joke on us. He is not telling us to think that we are in this new position of victory when we are actually not. Notice the words "in Christ Jesus our Lord." Through the cross, we are indeed in Christ. We don't move away from the gospel after we are converted, we live through its power!

Let me stay on this point a moment longer. Here is another important concept tied to the cross. The continual intercession of Jesus Christ is based on his crosswork. As we focus on the gospel, we realize that we are secure because Christ ever lives to intercede for us (Hebrews 7:25). How did he obtain this position? How could he take his place as our great high priest? He entered into this ministry on the basis of his death on the cross (Hebrews 9:12)! So our Christian life does not move from the gospel to service. Our service is connected to the gospel. We operate through his power. We must stay focused on the gospel. Our lives need gospel depth. It is only through the power of the gospel that we can minister and be an encouragement to God's people. I urge you not to let the familiarity with some of these words hinder you from getting the meaning of this truth. The gospel is not just for the lost! The gospel is at the very center of the entirety of the Christian life.

SALVATION IS IN THREE TENSES

This is a huge truth that must overcome a lot of preconceived ideas. Let me state the truth clearly. Then, I will go over why it is so difficult in many modern evangelical circles for this truth to register. Then finally, I will discuss its great implications. First of all, the New Testament clearly speaks of salvation as having a past, present, and future aspect to it. Now, here comes the really hard part. As a believer, your ultimate salvation is yet to come. The final stage of our salvation is future glorification. This glorification is the end of our *grace race* so to speak. We will receive resurrected, glorified bodies. We will enter into the fullness of God's kingdom. Redemption will be complete. The difficult part for believers to understand is that to be finally saved (saved in the future sense of the redemptive process), believers need to persevere in the faith. I am not saying that a genuine believer's future glorification is in jeopardy. I am saying that real believers keep the faith. Why is this truth that is clearly taught in Scripture so hard for many believers to assimilate into their Christian lives? I think that there are two reasons. The first reason is that in our Christian jargon we speak of salvation in only one tense—past. "I was saved when I was so many years old." "I got saved three weeks ago." And so on.

It is important to understand that the New Testament also often speaks of salvation this way (Ephesians 2:8; 2Timothy 1:9; Titus 3:5). But it is also important to understand that the New Testament also speaks of salvation as an ongoing and future event as well. It is important for believers to understand that God is still at work saving us. This does not mean that we are continually being justified. Justification is truly a one-time event whereby God declares us righteous based on what Christ did on the cross. However, all the parts of salvation are important and necessary. Thus, Paul speaks of salvation as an ongoing work in 1 Corinthians 1:18: "For the message of the cross is foolishness to those who are perishing, but to us who are being saved it is the power of God." God is continuing our deliverance from sin. We have clearly not yet arrived (2 Corinthians 1:10). It is clear also that salvation is spoken of as yet future (Romans 5:9–10; 1Corinthians 5:5).

This brings us to the crucial point of perseverance. As I briefly discuss this, I do not want to be misunderstood. Salvation is by God's grace—all of salvation. When I speak of perseverance, I am not implying that the salvation of true believers is not secure. It is secure. It is secure because of Christ's faithfulness (Philippians 1:6). But the same Bible that teaches security also teaches perseverance.[2] This means that real believers keep the faith. They do not ultimately fall away. It doesn't mean that real believers are perfect. No, we are still very much imperfect. It does not mean that we will not struggle with sin. No, we struggle with sin (although we

2. For a great study of perseverance, including a very helpful explanation of the warning passages in Scripture see Schreiner and Caneday, *The Race Set Before Us*.

struggle from a position of victory). It does not mean that we will not experience lapses of faith or that our faith will not indeed be very weak at times. It means that we experience God's grace in perseverance. He perseveres with us! A wonderful few verses in Luke's gospel can help us understand the issue. In Luke 22: 31–34, we have Peter boasting about being ready to die for Jesus Christ. At this moment, if Peter were going to write a hymn, he might have titled it "I Am Able." Peter, in this instance, was a classic example of a self-reliant believer. We know that when Peter's words were put to the test, he failed miserably. Perseverance does not mean that the testings, trials, and temptations of the Christian life are negated. However, do not miss God's grace in perseverance in the Luke passage. Think deeply on Luke 22:31–32: "And the Lord said, 'Simon, Simon! Indeed, Satan has asked for you, that he may sift *you* as wheat. But I have prayed for you, that your faith should not fail; and when you have returned to *Me*, strengthen your brethren.'" Peter will ultimately persevere in spite of some setbacks. His faith will not utterly fail. He will not completely fall away. Why? Because he is very clever? Because he is such a spiritual giant? No! Because of Jesus Christ's praying for him. We persevere by grace. Nonetheless, real believers do persevere. Those who actually do fall away completely from the faith simply evidence the fact that they did not have genuine faith in the first place (1 Corinthians 11:18–19; I John 2:19).

How does this help us? It compels us to continue to look to God's grace and not our own strength and merit. It keeps us from presumptuous positions like the one that says: "It doesn't matter what I do or how I live since I am already saved." It encourages us because we know that God is faithful and working in every moment of our lives. Our point however in this book is that it humbly moves us to exalt God and glory in him alone. There must never be a "look what I have done!" or "look what I am doing!" attitude. We persevere because of God's grace and for God's glory.

WE GROW BY GOSPEL NOURISHMENT NOT BY RULES OR "HOW TO" MESSAGES

Some time ago, I was asked to do a workshop at a Christian conference. My wife was also asked to speak to the ladies in a workshop. We taught one session each but also attended the main sessions which featured only one speaker. He spoke three or four times. He was very dynamic. He dealt with many relevant subjects. He seemed well informed in terms of some of the ungodly cultural influences of our time. He used a lot of Scripture. He was very convicting. After the conference, I heard a lot of positive comments as to this man's messages. When I got in my car to go home, I told my wife that I felt that something about the speaker's messages was drastically wrong. We both agreed that we did not want to be critical or negative, but to be honest, I just couldn't let it go. After some time and thought, I came to realize the problem. I also know that I am not alone in my assessment. The problem was that this particular preacher dealt with every issue by telling believers what to do. Now, you might be thinking that that sounds right! Of course, preachers ought to tell Christians how to live. He told these people how to have victory over pornography, how to know God's will, how to have victory over other sins, how to manage time wisely, etc.—all without the cross, God's grace, God's power, our total dependence. It was as if all we needed were a bunch of steps and we would be able to have victory (just like he had). *How to* preaching is really nothing but legalism. It can cause one of two things. Either it will stir up our self-righteousness if we think that we too are doing all of the right steps successfully. Or it will frustrate us because no matter how hard we try we cannot seem to successfully get it all together. I am not saying that there is no place in preaching for instruction or correction. There certainly is. I am saying that it must be accompanied by the truths of the gospel. We must see our inability and recognize God's ability. We do not have it altogether. We most certainly will not get it all together by simply following some steps or getting tough or by doing things in our own strength. Paul recognized that he was not sufficient to do anything of himself (2 Corinthians 3:5). He also recognized that what he did achieve was by the active, dynamic working of grace (1 Corinthians 15:10). We will not be ok if merely given steps and *how to* messages. We grow by being fed with the grace of God through the work of Jesus Christ. Hebrews 13:9 puts it this way: "Do not be carried about with various and strange doctrines. For *it is* good that the heart be established by grace, not with foods which have not profited those who have been occupied with them." In other words, believers need their hearts strengthened with grace not legalistic dietary laws or anything legalistic at all for that matter. Now I know some Christians who have rightly rejected ministries in which a certain preacher's standards form the basis for living the Christian life. These ministries tend to be narrow, militant, and arrogant. However, it doesn't matter whether the standards are yelled out nice and loud in a pulpit-pounding hyper-dogmatic message or if they are given more gently as some how-to things to consider doing so you can live a really great life. Without gospel-saturation, these kind of messages are actually dead.

As a believer, your soul must be nourished with the great truths about Jesus Christ. He is at the center of the whole Bible. He is the hero of every story. He is the one who gives and sustains life in your soul. Spiritual growth is God's work too. We must cooperate, it is true. But even our part is only possible because of God's part. Grace is the definitive element. It is because of God's part that we will ultimately do our part. This is why God is to receive all the glory—because it is his work from start to finish.

WHAT THESE TRUTHS POINT TO

Now that we have briefly covered these five significant truths, I hope that you can see their importance. I have certainly not exhausted all of the great and significant gospel truths in Scripture. I recognize that these truths we have discussed can be put many various ways. No matter how they are explained, if they are explained Biblically, they serve to point us directly to a God-centered approach to the Christian life. It is a life that calls us to glorify God. In the rest of this book, we will expand our explanation of God's glory and our duty to live for him. In one way or another, these five truths will always be a factor. It is my prayer that you will spend some time meditating on God as the supreme, sovereign, transcendent being that he is. May you behold his greatness, glory, perfection, power, and beauty. When you recognize God's transcendent greatness, it becomes that much more amazing that it is this God who pays attention to his fallen creatures. Consider Isaiah 57:15: "For thus says the High and Lofty One Who inhabits eternity, whose name *is* Holy: 'I dwell in the high and holy *place,* With him *who* has a contrite and humble spirit, To revive the spirit of the humble, And to revive the heart of the contrite ones.'" The first part of this verse certainly speaks to the greatness of God above his creation. Notice, however, the second part. God draws close to fallen humanity. By his grace, he brings people to himself. He allows us to know his greatness. He dwells with his created beings. In itself, this is a wondrous thing. However, when one considers that God does this to rebellious sinful people, it is truly amazing beyond measure. God saves us that we might know him. This is the ultimate goal of the gospel—God himself! God's work is bringing unworthy and undeserving human beings to himself through Jesus Christ that they might glorify and enjoy him forever. It is only as we see his supreme glory that we appreciate his amazing grace.

3

Defining God's Glory

WE HAVE looked at some huge truths that essentially mandate that we be God-centered. These truths point to his greatness and our dependence. They tell us that this transcendent God, who has no needs at all, nonetheless brought us into existence that we might know him. The next two chapters are inextricably linked together. In this chapter, we will talk about God's glory—who he is. In chapter 4, we will discuss man's duty—to glorify God. There is an important connection between the two. This chapter helps us to see that God is truly worthy to be made much of. The next chapter tells us that making much of God is exactly what we have been created to do. So now let's spend some time thinking about what God's glory is all about.

When thinking about God, it is helpful to look at different aspects of God separately. We call these different aspects of God's greatness and character his attributes. I must warn you of a danger here. Although it is extremely worthwhile to study God's attributes individually, we must never view God as simply a collection of attributes added together. To do this is to destroy God's unity of being. Instead, we must see God as a personal being whose attributes are all manifested in perfect harmony. We must seek to know God in his wholeness. He is not divided into parts. Yet, at the same time, each attribute helps us to see him more clearly. So understand that God is not divided into parts. His love does not fight against his wrath. He is never inconsistent with his own character. His being includes all his attributes exercised in perfect harmony with each other. He is a personal being who is supremely above all else. Because he is God, we will not be able to fully comprehend him. Do not let this stop you from trying to know him as fully as you can. He has graciously revealed himself to us through his Word and ultimately through his Son (John 1:18; Hebrews 1:2–3). Though our knowledge will certainly be imperfect, it can be real. It is God's will that we know him and glorify him. In this chapter, we will specifically deal with only one of God's attributes—his glory. The reason for specifically dealing with this attribute is because God's glory is a *summary* attribute. This means that it speaks of God's whole being. It refers to him in his fullness—all the attributes together. God is all-powerful, all-knowing, all-wise, eternal, merciful, good, etc. These are all individual attributes. When we speak of God's glory, all of God is in view. All of his attributes are included. We are saying that God is glorious through and through. There is no part of him that is not glorious. There is no bad side, no blemish, and no part that is not absolutely wonderful. Think of how different this is from what our natural tendencies would be in our thoughts toward God. One of our natural tendencies would be for us to recognize God's love as glorious but not God's wrath. We would think God is glorious when he forgives but not when he severely judges sin. But when we speak of God's glory, we are saying that God in his wholeness is glorious. His love is glorious, and his wrath is glorious. Every part of his being is glorious, and they all work together gloriously! His glory is not a separate attribute but really an expression of all of his unsurpassed greatness and holy character. Let's explore this for a little while.

GOD'S GLORY IS THE UNSURPASSED GREATNESS, MAJESTY, AND OUTSHINING OF HIS PERSON

When we speak of God's glory, we mean that every part of his being is fully great. We mean that his being and ways are majestic (or grand or magnificent). We mean that this great and majestic character is manifested in everything that God does. We mean that there is nothing equal to God or his works in the entire universe. Let's see how the Scriptures speak of this. The psalmist writes, "And blessed *be* his glorious name forever! And let the whole earth be filled *with* his glory. Amen and Amen" (Psalm 72:19). When the Psalmist speaks of God's glorious name, he is referring to all that God is. The Hebrews used the concept of one's name to refer to one's character, one's person. God's name is glorious! The prayer is that the whole earth would be filled with expressions of all that God is. In Colossians 1:11, Paul refers to God's "glorious power." The word "power" used by Paul refers to a force or strength that gives one supremacy of control, a ruling power. God's power is glorious. It is unsurpassed. Psalm 113: 4 says, "The LORD *is* high above all nations, his glory above the heavens." Here, God's glory is expressed in the idea of God's high, exalted position above all of his creation. I hope you are getting the picture. The

Scriptures speak of God's glory as the all-encompassing awesomeness of God. There are times when the Bible uses the word *glory* simply to refer to the honor that is due his name. We will certainly get to that in the next chapter. However, in the above verses we see a meaning to God's glory that goes beyond this. The verses mentioned are just a few that speak of God's glory as a kind of summary of the greatness of his being.

GOD'S GLORY IS SOMETIMES EXPRESSED BY AN UNEQUALLED BRIGHTNESS THAT SURROUNDS THE REVELATION OF HIMSELF

At times in Scripture, there is a brightness that surrounds manifestations of God. This brightness is a kind of illustration of God's unsurpassed glory. We see it when the angels appeared to the shepherds on the night of Jesus Christ's birth. Luke 2:9 states, "And behold, an angel of the Lord stood before them, and the glory of the Lord shone around them, and they were greatly afraid." Notice that it is the "glory of the Lord" that is shining forth. Again, this is a visible expression of God's majesty and greatness. In the New Jerusalem, there will be no need for the sun for the glory of God will give that holy place its light (Revelation 21:23). Peter, James, and John got a glimpse of this visible manifestation of God's being when Christ was transfigured before their eyes. The Scripture tells us that Jesus' "face shone like the sun, and his clothes became white as the light" (Matthew 17:2). When Peter testifies of this event, he speaks of the "Excellent Glory" (2 Peter 1:17). The word "excellent" refers to something magnificent. The point is that this shinning is suitable to the character that it represents. This unique and unequalled brightness points us to the true greatness of God's character. There is no one like God. He is infinitely above all else. His goodness is pure. His love is perfect. This great brightness is the outward expression of the magnificence of God alone. This outward, visible brightness simply illustrates the excellence that belongs to God intrinsically.

JESUS CHRIST MANIFESTED GOD'S GLORY IN HIS WORDS AND WORKS

If you want to see God's glory unfolded in a very real and compelling way, all you have to do is look at Jesus Christ. God's glory is so great that if we were to see it manifested in its fullness in our present mortal state, we would perish. When Moses asked God to show him his glory, God responded, "You cannot see My face; for no man shall see Me, and live" (Exodus 33:20). Thus God showed Moses a very partial revelation of his glory. That is what John means in his gospel when he says that no one has ever seen God (John 1:18). No one has ever seen a full manifestation of God in his glory. In our natural state, we would not survive such a revelation! Continuing in John 1:18, John makes this amazing statement: "The only begotten Son, who is in the bosom of the Father, he has declared *him*." The word "declare" refers to making something fully known by giving a detailed explanation. We get the word *to exegete* from this Greek word. In other words, Jesus Christ unfolds God's glory to us. He "exegetes" His Father! He makes God the Father clear to us. If we really want to behold the glory of God, we can see it in Jesus Christ. After Jesus performed his first miracle (turning water into wine), these words are recorded: "This beginning of signs Jesus did in Cana of Galilee, and manifested his glory; and his disciples believed in him" (John 2:11). Christ's miracle (or sign) pointed the disciples to his glory which, of course, reflected perfectly God the Father's glory. So when we speak of God's glory, we must understand that we see it as fully as we can possibly see it in the person of Jesus Christ!

THE ULTIMATE EXPRESSION OF GOD'S GLORY: THE CROSS

If we behold God's glory in the person and work of Jesus Christ, we must certainly focus our attention on the very heart of that work. God's glory is without doubt manifested in his creation. Psalm 19:1 makes it clear that "The heavens declare the glory of God; And the firmament shows his handiwork." However, creation with all of its God-glorifying wonders cannot be fully enjoyed unless it is redeemed. God's fallen creatures cannot truly know him, enjoy him, and enter into his presence unless they are rescued from sin and made new. This involves the most glorious work of the cross. The ultimate expression of God's glory is the cross of Jesus Christ. Through the cross alone do fallen creatures enter into the presence and joy of the Lord. In John 12:23, when Jesus said that it was time for the Son of Man to be glorified, he was not simply referring to his resurrection and ascension. He was speaking of being glorified in the cross through which he would save a people unto himself. Remember that the cross was not a temporary defeat while the resurrection of Jesus was the permanent victory. The cross was where victory took place as God's wrath toward sin was satisfied. The resurrection declared the victory. The resurrection was the prize that the victory on the cross secured, but victory happened on the cross. Jesus bought the salvation of all who believe in his atoning death. When the cross is in view, God's greatness shines forth. When we meditate on the cross of Christ, we should see in it our great sinfulness. Think about the fact that God had to sacrifice his own Son in death. Consider the wrath for sin that Christ had to bear—wrath that we deserved. At the same time, we must meditate on God's great love, mercy, compassion, and grace. We should be in great wonder at the fact that God should give himself up in death for us. This is what we should see when we come humbly to the cross. We should see the greatness of our own sinfulness. We also should see the enormity of God's great love in its fullness. We see a love incomprehensible. We see holiness lifting up the defiled and wretched. We see the ultimate sacrifice—God sacrificing his only Son. We see the ultimate glory. No wonder that Paul cried out, "But God forbid that I should boast except in the cross of our Lord Jesus Christ, by whom the world has been crucified to me, and I to the world" (Galatians 6:14).

GOD DESIRES THAT HE BE KNOWN IN HIS GLORY

Now, that we have had a brief look at this summary attribute, we are ready to see how it completely must shape our lives. If we have been truly touched by God's glory, it must make a drastic difference in how we think and live. Let me close with just some of the implications of God's glory for our lives. Some of the following points will be covered in more detail later in the book.

1. We must grow in the knowledge of his glory. We need to see it more and more fully. We do this by seeing Christ in all of Scripture. Scripture is Christo-centric. That means that the whole Bible is about Jesus Christ. We must continually search the Scriptures and behold Christ's glory (2 Corinthians 3:18). I am suggesting that believers must stop playing games with God's revelation of his glory. We must seek to know Jesus Christ. We must meditate on God's Word. We must understand that the Bible is not just a rule book. Yes, there is law in the Bible. But the law is pointing out our sinfulness so that we can then turn to God's grace through Christ. Thus, the Bible is most importantly a gospel book. We desperately need to see God in all of his glory through Jesus Christ.

2. We must worship God in all of the expressions of his glory. We must see his greatness in the expressions of his justice as well as in the expressions of his mercy. We must be still and recognize that he alone is God and he alone is worthy to be worshipped (Revelation 19:1–3; Ephesians 1:6). Worship must be in and entertainment must go out. Corporate worship must be centered around God's glory. He must be the focus. We must prepare our hearts. We must prepare our bodies by getting the proper rest before worship. We must prepare our souls by praying for our corporate worship services. In our private lives, we must realize that God is glorious and thus worthy to be constantly praised. We must live in the spirit of thankfulness to God.

3. We must see the need for self-glory to be eliminated. There is only one God. He must be exalted, not us.

We are fallen, sinful creatures who deserve eternal destruction. How can we stand before anyone and proclaim our own greatness. Exalting anything else is idolatry, including ourselves. (Psalm 148:13; Romans 1:21–23). Let's look up to God and then down to ourselves. Let's understand ourselves in the light of God's glory. We must remember that God resists the proud (2 Peter 5:5). He hates pride (Proverbs 6:16–17). We have every reason to be humble. Truly self-glory must go. It must also go in the way that we rear our children. Self-esteem psychology in child-rearing helps young people to learn to make much of themselves. They learn to exalt themselves above all else. We must show our children a vision of a glorious God.

4. We must see God's glory in such a way that it brings us the ultimate joy of life. He must be our treasure because he is, in fact, the supreme treasure (Psalm 16:11). God brings us to a knowledge of his glory so that we can enjoy him eternally. He desires us to be brought to his glory that we might behold it forever (John 17:24). But even right now during our life in this fallen world, he wants us to be filled with joy in Jesus Christ (I Peter 1:8). Believers must stop seeking to be satisfied with the things of this world that can never truly satisfy and start seeking satisfaction in the only one who can truly satisfy our souls—the glorious God.

At this point, we are ready to move on and talk about our duty to live for God's glory. How do we do this? What does it mean? What does a God-centered life really look like? This is the subject of our next chapter.

4

Our Ultimate Aim: To Glorify God

NOW THAT we have looked at what God's glory is, we are ready to look at our duty—to glorify him. Let me begin by taking any negativity out of the word *duty*. Glorifying God is not to be thought of as drudgery. If it is drudgery, then it does not glorify God! I hope that this will become clear as our discussion goes on, but I feel like it is important from the beginning to understand this. Yes, it is our absolute duty to glorify God. No, this is not an unpleasant experience at all. On the contrary, it is the most fulfilling experience in the universe. I am not saying that living for God's glory is easy. I am not saying that living for God's glory means not experiencing any pain and suffering. I am saying that in glorifying God there is a fullness of joy at the very core of our being. God is the object of it and in him we delight. So from now on, if I use the word *duty*, read it with the concept of *delight* built in!

One more important item needs to be stated before getting into the main emphasis of this chapter. When I speak about glorifying God, please understand that we do this by God's grace alone. Glorifying God is not conjuring up some very impressive works by our own self-effort to impress God with. Our own self-effort will have the very opposite effect. We will begin to operate on a system of merit to impress God. This will glorify us and not God! Let me see if I can put this very simply. A believer must never say something like this: "I am very proud that I have been able to glorify God in my life!" I truly hope you see the great mistake of that statement. Pride is not something that God considers a virtue. In fact, God hates pride (Proverbs 6:16, 17). Consider well what James 4:6 says: "But He gives more grace. Therefore He says: 'God resists the proud, But gives grace to the humble.'" So please understand that we glorify God through His grace. Otherwise, we would be glorifying ourselves.

Now, before we try to define glorifying God in practical terms, let's begin with the totality of this concept of glorifying God. What I am trying to say is that God must be at the very center of our lives. It must be all about him. This idea of God being at the center is really foreign to our culture. But it goes beyond that. It is really foreign to the unregenerate heart of man. David Wells expresses this so well in his book *The Courage to be Protestant*. Wells states that our culture has lost its center. "Why has life lost its center? The biblical answer explains why all of life has become disordered. As the twenty-first century is beginning in the West, part of that disorder is the sense that life has no center, that it is adrift, and that it has no meaning. This answer, which explains all of this, is sin. And this is the normative answer. It does not change. This, in every age, is the answer that explains life's disorder."[1] Wells goes on to explain the particular effects of sin in our culture. He states that in our postmodern era God has been displaced by the haunting non-virtue of meaningless. He writes, "The self that has

1. Wells, *The Courage to be Protestant*, 99.

been made to bear the weight of being the center of all reality, the source of all our meaning, mystery, and morality, finds that it has become empty and fragile."[2] The real and glorious God is replaced by that which can never ultimately fulfill. Due to the fall and man's subsequent corruption, man is quite frankly, man-centered. Paul expresses it like this in Romans 1:21–23: "Because, although they knew God, they did not glorify *him* as God, nor were thankful, but became futile in their thoughts, and their foolish hearts were darkened. Professing to be wise, they became fools, and changed the glory of the incorruptible God into an image made like corruptible man—and birds and four-footed animals and creeping things." What a picture of the rejection of God-centeredness! God's glory was not acknowledged. There was no thanksgiving to God. Man thought that his foolishness was wisdom, but his heart was in spiritual darkness. God was dethroned, and man was placed at the center. Do you see the problem? More than that, do you feel the problem? Does it grieve you that mankind has universally rejected God's rule and not seen his glory? As believers, we must see the need for God to be at the center in order that we might begin to turn it around in our own hearts by God's grace. So I want to point out here three areas that we must exercise care in.

WE MUST BE CAREFUL TO AVOID THE TRIVIALIZATION OF GOD

We trivialize God when we are presented with awesome thoughts about his person and work and say, "That's great; now let's move on to more important things, *like me!*" In

2. Ibid., 112.

presenting the gospel to people, it is very difficult to get people to truly understand the implications of their sinfulness. Many times, one hears a "So what, I'm a sinner, so is everyone else" attitude. When we speak of God's glory, we must not respond with "So what—no big deal." It is a big deal. That's the point. It is central. It is the biggest deal! Romans 11:36 speaks directly to the centrality of God's glory. It reads, "For of him and through him and to him *are* all things, to whom *be* glory forever. Amen." God ordains all things ("of him"), sustains all things ("through him"), and is the ultimate goal of all things ("to him"). Do not miss the last of these three magnificent facts. It means he is at the very center of the universe. All things point to him. He is to be glorified in all things. He must be worshipped. He is worthy to receive all honor and praise. He must not be trivialized. Someday all will know and bow down (Philippians 2:11). Someday, no one will trivialize God. As believers we ought to get the point right now! Can Christians and churches trivialize God? I believe so. In fact, I think this goes on more frequently than we realize. I do not think I am being sensationalistic or exaggerating when I say that it is prevalent in contemporary Western evangelicalism. We see it in the shallowness of the songs that are sung. We see it in the lack of theological understanding of the average Christian. We see it in the casual response to sin in the lives of believers. We see it in the misunderstanding of God's grace. We see it in the replacing of God's ordained means of spiritual life and growth with man-made schemes and programs. We certainly must evaluate our lives and be careful that we are not guilty of making very little of the God who is worthy of making very much of.

WE MUST BE CAREFUL NOT TO MAKE LIGHT OF THE CROSS

The writer of Hebrews warns: "How shall we escape if we neglect so great a salvation" (Hebrews 2:3). Without a long explanation of the warning passages in Scripture, suffice it to say that this verse means that we should understand just how great a salvation we have been given and we should, therefore, make living for the glory of God the main event of our lives! Christ's redemptive work removes the obstacles of sin and condemnation, so that we can see God's glory (Romans 8:1; 2 Corinthians 4:6). We have the privilege of relating to God through our position in Jesus Christ, all because of his crosswork. We never stand in our own righteousness before God. If we ever did, we would be completely unacceptable. Through Christ alone, we have been made acceptable (Ephesians 1:6). Because of the cross, we have a new heart (2 Corinthians 5:17) and the indwelling presence of the Holy Spirit (Romans 8:9). We now have new desires and a new power residing within our souls! We now have access to his throne. But all these things are on the basis of Christ's work on the cross. This must always be before us. We must not make light of Christ's death on the cross on our behalf. We must pursue God passionately. We must seek to glorify him with all of our hearts!

WE MUST BE CAREFUL NOT TO COMPARTMENTALIZE OUR SPIRITUAL LIFE

By this, I mean that we must not be spiritual on Sunday in church and neglect living for God's glory the rest of the week. We must not make a joyful noise unto the Lord during the worship service, and celebrate with worldliness the rest of the time. As I write these words, I am about to take a full week's vacation. I am looking forward to it. I will be away from my church and my ministry. But I will not be vacationing from my Christianity! Spiritual life is a full time business. More importantly, our relationship with God is a full time relationship. All of our lives must glorify God. Paul makes this very clear in 1 Corinthians 10:31: "Therefore, whether you eat or drink, or whatever you do, do all to the glory of God." I once read a devotional by John Piper about how to drink orange juice for the glory of God.[3] I have pretty much forgotten his actual words, but I got the point. He was simply explaining what Paul meant. Everything is to be done for God's glory. Everything is actually a spiritual issue. I remember talking once to a acquaintance who was very upset because he went to a spiritual retreat and they had a speaker who discussed finances. My friend remarked that he wished that they had kept the discussion focused on spiritual matters. He did not see that one's finances are a spiritual matter. Everything is a spiritual matter! The question is not only "What's in your wallet?" The real issue is how you are using what's in your wallet. How are you living at work, play, school, in the home? We must be serious about glorifying our great God. We must not compartmentalize our spiritual life.

WHAT EXACTLY DOES LIVING FOR GOD'S GLORY MEAN?

With the above in mind, let's now develop a practical definition of glorifying God. Let me begin by a personal illustra-

3. Piper, *Pierced by the Word*, 28.

tion. Growing up I was a big sports fan. I was never a good athlete, but I loved watching sports, especially baseball, football, and basketball. When I was a teenager (yes, many years ago!), I began to enjoy ice hockey as well. The big attraction was a very young defenseman for the Boston Bruins named Bobby Orr. He was amazing. He literally changed the game of hockey. Watching Orr play was electrifying. I certainly thought so. Just ask my wife. When we were dating, I would pick her up at her house, drive back to my house, and make this poor young lady sit through just about every game. I am not the one to ask about creative dating! You might say I was somewhat obsessed with watching Bobby Orr play hockey. Now how does this relate to living for God's glory? Well, during my days as a Bobby Orr fan, he dominated many of my conversations. Of course, everywhere people followed hockey, he dominated many a conversation in his day. He was, at the time, the talk of the sport. He was held in highest esteem by just about everyone who knew the game of hockey. We hockey fans spent our time making much of him. Unfortunately, our sports heroes and entertainment figures do become like gods to their fans. This is not a good thing at all, but it certainly can help us understand what it means to glorify God. Transfer all of that excitement, talk, time, and obsession to the one who really deserves it and you can start to get the picture. To glorify God we essentially give God what he is due because of his inherent glory (what we talked about in the last chapter)! Because he is God, glorious, great, perfect, beautiful, majestic, holy, sovereign, etc., we esteem him supremely above all else. Because we esteem him supremely above all else, it affects every part of our lives. *We spend our time making much of him!* We live for him. To make it simple, we make a big deal about God—the biggest deal about God. To flesh this idea out a little more, here are some foundational aspects of glorifying God.

WE EXALT HIM

"Be exalted, O God, above the heavens; *Let* Your glory *be* above all the earth" (Psalm 57:5). To exalt God is to bring him up to the level that he is truly at in our own hearts, minds, words, and deeds. In other words, we don't actually bring him up at all for he is already infinitely high above all else—he is supreme. When we exalt him, we are acknowledging that he is supreme and living like he is supreme. True exaltation comes from our hearts, and then proceeds out of our mouths, and finally into our lives.

WE MAGNIFY HIM

"Oh, magnify the LORD with me, And let us exalt his name together" (Psalm 34:3). Magnifying God is much like exalting him. The magnification being spoken of in this Psalm means a promoting or a making powerful. Again, we do not make God more powerful or promote him to a higher rank. What we can do is proclaim his power and rank. We can declare it to others and tell of his mighty works. We can show forth by our words and works just how powerful and above all God really is. We give God the credit for creating this world by His mighty power. We acknowledge that God sustains this world. We recognize that our existence is from him. He is the source of life and its sustainer. We see his power behind all of nature. We see his power behind all of history. We bow down before him and recognize our dependence upon him alone.

WE RECOGNIZE HIS GLORY IN SUCH A WAY THAT WE DESIRE HIM

"As the deer pants for the water brooks, So pants my soul for You, O God" (Psalm 42:1). To pant for God as a deer would pant for the water brooks speaks of having a great thirst to know God in a fuller way. It speaks of a yearning to be in his presence, an intense desire for God himself. This is a vital part of glorifying God. In fact, if there is something we desire above him, he is not glorified. On a human level, I would be very disappointed to say the least, if I knew my wife desired to be with someone else more than me. On the other hand, when she tells me she missed me if I have been away from her for even a short time, it makes me feel great. Our desire for God shows his value in our hearts. It exalts and magnifies his name. It says that he is the treasure of our hearts. He must be our supreme treasure if we are to truly live for his glory.

WE RECOGNIZE THAT HE IS ABSOLUTELY PERFECT IN HIS BEING AND WORKS

"*He is* the Rock, his work *is* perfect; For all his ways *are* justice, A God of truth and without injustice; Righteous and upright *is* he" (Deuteronomy 32:4). God is glorified when with our whole hearts we recognize his perfections. When we discussed God's glory, we said that it was a summary attribute. It is a way of saying that God in his fullness is completely perfect. Now, it is one thing to say God is glorious and perfect. It is another thing to actually have it in one's heart at all times. It is this heart that trusts God's perfect works and ways that brings glory to God. When things are going well, it is easy to praise God. What happens when things do not go well? What happens when horrible things happen in one's life? God expects us to know that he is still on his throne, his promises are still in effect, he is still accomplishing his sovereign and good purposes, and we are still to exalt and magnify him! Exalting God through very difficult times is a defining characteristic in a life that glorifies God.

Not too long ago, I preached that when a believer is physically ill, the primary goal is not to get well but to glorify God. I was, of course, not saying that we should not seek medical attention or that we should not pray for healing. It is quite normal to desire to be physically well. We do not have to pretend that bad things are good things to glorify God. We must simply recognize that God uses the bad things to bring about his sovereignly good purposes. What I was saying is that our priority in life doesn't change when our circumstances do. So, when a believer is not physically well, he must still recognize that God is not making a mistake. He has not abdicated his throne. He has not stopped working in one's life. He is still God. We must still glorify him. His ways are perfect even when it would not seem so. It was not long after I preached this theme in a church service that a woman in our church was diagnosed with terminal cancer. It was a sudden and shocking diagnosis. She only lived a few months after her cancer was discovered. During that time, she asked me to visit with her for she had some questions.

During my visit, she not only reminded me of the message I had preached about glorifying God in one's illness, she also told me that glorifying God was exactly what she wanted to do! In that room, at that moment, I thought, "Here is real Christianity! Here is the reality of Jesus Christ in one's heart!" I praise God that she did glorify him through this battle with approaching death. This woman inspired me with her life, but deeply touched me in her death. She did not get well, but she did go home. Her death was gain as she departed to be with Christ (Philippians 1:21–23). God did not make a mistake in her life. He brought glory to his name and brought one of his children home to be in his presence awaiting resurrection day! We must recognize that God is the perfect one. We are so finite. He is infinitely great. We certainly do not understand all his ways. We need to trust in his sovereign goodness and glorify him.

SO MUCH MORE

There is so much more involved in glorifying God. The above are just some basics. All believers are still learning and growing in this life of glorifying God. He is worthy. We must continue our pursuit of knowing him. As we move on in this book, we will now look more closely at what living for God's glory looks like. We will examine some specific issues and situations. We must talk more about God's grace, our need for humility, and the concept of breaking the power of self-glory. This subject will never be exhausted. God's glory has infinite dimensions (though I promise you, this book does not!). Believers will actively glorify God throughout eternity. When it comes to God's glory, there is always more . . . so much more.

5

God: The Object Not Simply
the Source of Our Joy

W E HAVE already mentioned briefly that the duty of living for the glory of God must not be thought of as drudgery but delight. This is because God should be the center of our lives, and in knowing him there is a joy that is absolute, permanent, and full. By absolute, I mean that it is joy in its essence. It is real. Joy in God is the only true joy. By permanent, I mean that no one can take this joy from us. God brings us to himself by grace, and he also brings his joy to our hearts. God is faithful to finish what he starts. We will know him forever, and thus we will know his joy forever. By full, I mean that there is nothing else that satisfies our souls but God. Human beings look to all kinds of places and do all kinds of things to find contentment, satisfaction, and fulfillment in their lives. The real thing comes only from knowing God through Jesus Christ. Again, I must remind you that all of this comes by grace through the person and work of Jesus Christ.

Jesus Christ died on the cross to save a people who would then have God as the object of their joy eternally. Let me explain more fully what I mean by this. Before the foundation of the world, the redemptive work of Christ was

planned to enable fallen men to come to the place of enjoying God by redeeming them from their sins. By enjoying
God, I mean that men would recognize him and behold
him in such a way that he would be the sole object of delight
to their souls. They might delight in other things but only
as they see him in those other things, only as those other
things reflect his glory. In other words, human happiness
would be God-centered. God is pleased when he is at the
center, when his creatures delight in him. This is all part of
glorifying God. Believers must understand that this joy in
God cannot happen apart from the cross—apart from salvation in Jesus Christ. In Christ's work, the power of self-glory
is broken. We are given a new heart. His Spirit is placed
within us. In the end (the ultimate goal of redemption),
God brings us to the place where we can be in his presence, experience him fully, and joy in him forever. In this
chapter, we want to deal with a potentially serious problem.
There can be a reversal of what God desires to happen in
one's relationship with him. Instead of one finding his joy
in Christ, some people seek to use Christ to find their joy in
other places. In other words, God is used as an asset to help
one find a worldly happiness instead of a God-centered joy.
This is what I mean when I speak of seeking God to be the
source of one's joy but not seeking him as the object of one's
joy. This is not simply some play on words. It is a serious
distortion of the gospel. Contemporary culture, some contemporary churches, and much of contemporary preaching
can actually foster this kind of relationship with God. Let's
try to see the problem more clearly in this chapter and in
the next we will look at some Biblical answers.

THE PROBLEM WHEN GOD IS THE SOURCE NOT THE OBJECT

Let me explain the essence of this problem by giving you a human example. I have been in active ministry for over twenty-eight years. In that time, I have been approached by many shall I say "shifty-looking" people asking me for money. What I am saying is that there have been many attempts to con me into giving out money under false pretenses. At first, I was very naïve about this sort of thing. Certainly, I thought, these people were genuine and sincere as they told me their troubles. The story oftentimes went something like this: "I need $52.85 (notice the exact amount) to take a bus to such and such a place because my mother (or father, brother, sister, aunt, best friend, etc.) is dying and I must see them before they depart from this world. The reason I don't have the money is because I just started a new job and I don't get paid until next Wednesday. I need to buy the bus ticket today and leave this afternoon (notice the urgency) so that I can visit my loved one and then be back on time to show up for work and not lose my job (notice how responsible they are). I am desperate. Of course, as soon as I get paid next Wednesday, I will pay you back the money. I have no where else to turn." The stories certainly varied. Some of them were very creative. But the bottom line was always the same. I (or the church I represented) was the last resort. If I didn't help (with money!), some tragic circumstance would definitely come to pass. I gave in to these people more than once. Call me a very slow learner. One thing is for sure—I have never given in to one of these situations in which I had reservations and found my reservations unfounded! In other words, promises made were never kept. I never saw these people again. I do not think that I am being too presumptuous in thinking that the money was actually used for something else (like alcohol or drugs). After many of these situations, I have now actually learned to ask more questions, propose different solutions to these kinds of problems, and make different offers than money. I have come to this conclusion: at least most of the time, the people who tell these kinds of stories are very good liars (please do not think me too unkind!). If you are not aware of it, these kinds of con games are a common place occurrence among those desperately trying to get money for drugs or alcohol. Now, here's the point of the illustration. To those I gave the money to, I became the source of their joy (their drugs, drink, etc.). But I was certainly not the object of their joy. The object was the drugs or drink! Now, forgive me for this long analogy but try to follow here. God is not glorified when we attempt to *use* him as our source for our own supposed joy in things. He is not glorified when we take him on in our lives as our supplier of self-glorying pleasures. He did not save us to become the Divine Supplier for our own self-perceived and lustful wants. This is a kind of Christianity in which God is the wish-granter for our *lusts*. Please don't misunderstand the use of the word *lusts* here. These lusts may simply be what we perceive as our real needs. They may not be evil in and of themselves. But in our lives they have become idols and have in a real sense replaced God as the source of our satisfaction. The idea here is that once we have the stuff, we move on to enjoy *it* and not God. This is just a subtle way of claiming to have God at the center but actually still having ourselves at the center. It is a self-glorifying relationship not a God-glorifying one. I believe that this kind of using God happens more often than we think. Now, I am not saying that God does not give us things to enjoy. I am saying that he must be much more than that to us as believers. I am saying that our longing must be for God himself. This is what the cross is all about. God must be the object of our joy not merely the source we look to for self-centered living.

GOD IS THE PERFECT OBJECT OF OUR JOY

Let's look briefly at how things ought to be; how things were created to be. God created us not out of his need but out of his fullness. By this, I mean, that God did not need us in order to be satisfied. He was perfectly satisfied in himself. Father, Son, and Holy Spirit enjoyed eternal pleasure in the love that they shared within themselves (John 17:5, 24). So he created human beings so that they could be brought into unity with himself and share in his fullness, love and joy (John 17:21, 26). God created human beings to give them the gift of himself! We must picture this eternal relationship that we have been brought into with the understanding that we are still the creatures and that God is still God. We do not become gods. We remain human beings. Our purpose is to know God, glorify God, and find perfect joy in his being. I confess, at this point, that I do not understand it all. I do know that the eternal glories that we have in God himself are what we were made for. I know that we were created for him and that we were created to have eternal pleasure in him. I know this because I Thessalonians 4:17 tells us that when Christ comes "We shall always be with the Lord." In addition, Psalm 16:11 tells us that "In [his] presence *is* fullness of joy; At [his] right hand *are* pleasures forevermore." So God in salvation graciously brings a people into his presence forever so that they may have eternal delight in him. Do you understand the gospel in this way? In his excellent book, *God Is the Gospel*, John Piper asks, "If you could have heaven, with no sickness, and with all the friends you ever had on earth, and all the food you ever liked, and all the leisure activities you ever enjoyed, and all the natural beauties you ever saw, all the physical pleasures you ever tasted, and no human conflict or any natural disasters, could you be satisfied with heaven, if Christ were not there?"[1] Piper's point is immensely important. Our ultimate delight is to be God himself not simply in some good things that we have from him. Salvation is about knowing and delighting in God. He does not need us, but we need him to be happy in the eternal and ultimate sense. Only God himself can bring us happiness. There is only happiness in God himself. What I am saying is that God is both the source and the object of our joy! Let me ask you to simply read the following verses that wonderfully express the joy to be found in God!

> **Psalm 43:4** Then I will go to the altar of God, To God my exceeding joy; And on the harp I will praise You, O God, my God.

> **Isaiah 29:19** The humble also shall increase *their* joy in the LORD, And the poor among men shall rejoice In the Holy One of Israel.

> **Habakkuk 3:18** Yet I will rejoice in the LORD, I will joy in the God of my salvation.

1. Piper, *God Is the Gospel*, 15.

Matthew 13:44 Again, the kingdom of heaven is like treasure hidden in a field, which a man found and hid; and for joy over it he goes and sells all that he has and buys that field.

Luke 10:20 Nevertheless do not rejoice in this, that the spirits are subject to you, but rather rejoice because your names are written in heaven."

John 15:11 These things I have spoken to you, that My joy may remain in you, and *that* your joy may be full.

Acts 13:52 And the disciples were filled with joy and with the Holy Spirit.

Romans 14:17 for the kingdom of God is not eating and drinking, but righteousness and peace and joy in the Holy Spirit.

Galatians 5:22 But the fruit of the Spirit is love, joy, peace, longsuffering, kindness, goodness, faithfulness,

Psalm 33:21 For our heart shall rejoice in him, Because we have trusted in his holy name.

Psalm 35:9 And my soul shall be joyful in the LORD; It shall rejoice in his salvation.

Isaiah 61:10 I will greatly rejoice in the LORD, My soul shall be joyful in my God; For he has clothed me with the garments of salvation, he has covered me with the robe of righteousness, As a bridegroom decks *himself* with ornaments, And as a bride adorns *herself* with her jewels.

Philippians 4:4 Rejoice in the Lord always. Again I will say, rejoice!

I realize that these verses mean even more when studied in their context. But even a simple reading of them helps us to know that God desires his children to have joy, and that God desires his children to have that joy in him. This is not some minor truth that you should relegate to the less important aspects of being a Christian. This is something of major importance. When God is not the object of our joy, we are living a distorted form of Christianity. We are certainly not exalting God. We are saying that he does not satisfy. You can be busy "serving" God and doing church stuff yet all the while looking for joy in all the wrong places. In fact, you may be serving with the mindset that you are earning rewards—things that will bring you happiness. It is so urgent for us to understand that God is the perfect object of one's joy. Before we move on to see some solutions to the problem of God not being the object of our joy, I want to share my concern over an expression that I frequently hear in testimonies that may actually be a problem instead of a praise.

"HE'S ALWAYS THERE FOR ME"

Have you ever heard someone praising God for "always being there for me"? I hear it a lot and am concerned because I think it is actually expressing a problem! This commonly heard expression is not blatantly false but is fraught with potential problems and misunderstandings. I point these problems out here for they go right along with the idea of God simply being seen as the source of one's joy. When someone uses the expression "God is always there for me," at least sometimes, they seem to mean that God is always there to meet their otherwise unmet needs as they seek to live out their own lives with their own self-centered goals. The problem is that we must not be driven by what we *perceive* as unmet needs. This places the focus on us. Life becomes what we want independently of God (except for the fact that we look to him to give us what we want). It would seem like Christ's call for one who is his disciple to "deny himself" and to "take up his cross" and "follow" Christ has been put out of view (Luke 9: 23). By the way, Jesus speaks of this cross-bearing as a "daily" or continuous way of living; it is not simply for once in a while. It is hard to reconcile the kind of life that Christ has actually called us to (one of sacrifice, surrender, commitment, suffering, etc.) with a life focused on unmet needs. Believers must see the Christian life in different terms. Allow me to use the phrase *joyful distresses* (see 2 Corinthians 12:10 where Paul states that he takes "pleasure in infirmities"). We must see the Christian life as a life in which we delight in Jesus Christ, and, as a result, desire to share in his sufferings for the kingdom of God (Philippians 3:10). So if "God is always there for me" means that he is always the source of my strength and the object of my joy, as I seek to live for his glory, then that's just fine. But it is obvious, in some contexts, that this is not what is meant.

This expression must certainly never be used to mean that God is always there to give me things that I should not desire in the first place! Do we really believe that the holy, righteous God of the gospel is there to grant us a carnal wish list? Do not the Scriptures call us to "abstain from fleshly lusts, which war against the soul" (1 Peter 2:11)? So "God is always there for me" can become an expression spoken out of our remaining sinfulness rather than an expression that is truly God-centered. Another idea that must never be conveyed in this expression is that God is always there for me to make much of me! When someone believes that it is important that God make much of them, then the gospel is truly being turned on its head. It is almost as if some Christians are saying that it is a good thing God makes much of them, otherwise they would have to look elsewhere, for they must be made much of! They would have to find someone else to fill them with themselves. Do you see how this goes against the very essence of why we exist? We exist to glorify God. We exist to delight in him and make much of him for he is worthy!

I would favor doing away with the expression "He is always there for me." We may certainly claim his promise that he will never leave or forsake us (Hebrews 13:5). We may certainly convey the truth that God is always working for our ultimate good and his ultimate glory (Romans 8:28). At the least let us make sure that we are not misunderstood in our testimonies. God is always there to show me more of his greatness, faithfulness, power, strength, goodness, love, and grace. He does this by showing me his worthiness. He shows me his sovereign rule. He shows me the knowledge of his glory in the face of Jesus Christ (2 Corinthians 4:6). He does this so that I will recognize the worth of his being, so that I will praise his Holy name. He truly meets my needs— my real needs. The truth we must see is this: *he is my real need.* I am to find my joy in his being. I am to delight in him and seek to display his glory. Whatever expressions we use, they must exalt him. Our great goal must be that which is expressed in Psalm 145:1–3: "I will extol You, my God, O King; And I will bless Your name forever and ever. Every day I will bless You, And I will praise Your name forever and ever. Great *is* the LORD, and greatly to be praised; And his greatness *is* unsearchable." In the next chapter, let's see why we actually can have God as the object of our joy. Then as the book moves on, let's look at some practical application of these truths.

6

Breaking the Power of Self-Glory

WE HAVE mentioned self-glory from time to time so far. It ought to be patently obvious that self-glory opposes God's glory. Remember the very first truth we discussed in chapter one: *you do not deserve to be saved.* It may help, at this time, to go back and read that section. In any event, from that truth flows this one: *you do not have anything to actually glory in regarding yourself.* Let me put this another way, but brace yourself, for this is a difficult truth indeed. We are all by virtue of our fallen nature fit vessels for God's condemnation. I do not say this lightly. Human beings are vessels of wrath in their unregenerate state. We become vessels of mercy solely by God's sovereign grace (John 3:36; Ephesians 2:3; Romans 9:22–23). Nonetheless, in one's flawed and fallen state, the tendency is to think highly of oneself not lowly. To give you some idea of our misconceptions, let me give you a perfectly wrong interpretation of some of Christ's own words. In Matthew 25:41, Jesus speaks of casting the unrighteous into the everlasting fire prepared for the devil and his angels. There are some things that must not be read into this verse. First, it is wrong to think that fallen sinful human beings do not really belong in hell, because it was prepared for Satan and his angels. If hell were an inappropriate punishment, do you not think that God could make another place more appropriate? He could and he would. Secondly, it is wrong to think that God is forced here into putting these sinners in hell by some kind of rule or law outside of his control. Some external law demands it, so God's hands are tied. No! There is no rule or law outside of God. He is transcendent. When God casts the unrighteous into hell, it is his own justice that is being carried out. Remember what we said in chapter one about God's self-existence. He did not evolve. He is not bound by anything outside of himself. He is acting in Matthew 25:41 in accordance with his perfect character. He is glorious in his judgment as well as in his mercy. Please do not miss this. He does not say: "Depart from me to hell for I do not have any other place to put you. I really made hell for Satan and his angels, but there is nothing I can do." Notice two words in the text of great significance: "you cursed". He is commanding their departure to hell because they are cursed. They are deserving sinners. He is saying that they are going to a place prepared for the devil and his angels because it is the kind of place that *is* appropriate for them. Now, here comes an important truth. Apart from God's grace, it is also an appropriate place for those of us who have been saved. It is only by God's great and rich mercy that we are saved! We must not drain the words *mercy* and *grace* of their significance. They speak to the fact that their recipients get something that they do not deserve while being spared of something that they do deserve. We deserve hell; we get heaven. We deserve separation from God forever; we get to spend eternity enjoying him. This condemnation is not pleasant. I assure you that

God himself takes no pleasure in it. The point is that he is acting in accordance with his purposes and character, not against them. God created mankind in his image so that human being could reflect God's glory. We are fallen, rebellious sinners who do not by nature do this. That is what Romans 3:23 means when it states, "For all have sinned and fall short of the glory of God." Consider for our discussion then this truth: *if we were fit vessels for hell, where does that leave room for self-glory?* Should we not glory only in the one who saved us from hell? We most certainly should (1 Corinthians 1:29–31)! I have gone through all of the above to make this point: the power of self-glory must be broken, if we are to glorify God and have him alone as the object of our joy. In the rest of this chapter, we will look at the problem more closely and we will see that the answer to the problem is found in the cross.

THE PROBLEM: THE UNREGENERATE HUMAN HEART LIKES SIN AND SELF-GLORY

There is no doubt that Scripture teaches that a heart that is dead to spiritual things still has desires, affections, and feelings. The problem is that these desires, affections, and feeling are for sinful things. Consider what Paul told the Ephesians about their pre-conversion state, "Among whom also we all once conducted ourselves in the lusts of our flesh, fulfilling the desires of the flesh and of the mind, and were by nature children of wrath, just as the others" (Ephesians 2:3). The unsaved are in bondage to their sinful nature. Therefore, when an unregenerate person sins, he is simply following his heart. It is important to understand that even desires and actions that have the outward appearance of goodness are inwardly corrupted by things like wrong motive, lack of love, self-glory, etc. There is no one in an unsaved state that has a pure heart or performs good deeds in God's sight (Romans 8:7, 8). Ultimately, the unsaved person is driven by the desires of his flesh. Jonathan Edwards, the great pastor-theologian of the 1700's, preached a sermon titled "The Justice of God in the Damnation of Sinners" during the Awakenings of 1734–1735. Although his message would be scorned by many in our modern culture, his words are just as true today as they were then. Listen to how he describes the hearts of mankind: "Yea, you have not only spent the time in worldly, vain, and unprofitable thoughts, but immoral thoughts; pleasing yourself with the reflection of past acts of wickedness, and in contriving new acts. Have you not spent much holy time in gratifying your lusts in your imaginations; yea, not only holy time, but the very time of public worship, when you have appeared in God's more immediate presence? How have you not only not attended to the worship, but have in the mean time been feasting your lusts, and wallowing yourself in abominable uncleanness!"[1] It is simply a fact of life—lost people, whether conscious of it or not, like sin, even in the midst of being religious. This does not mean that lost people like every kind of sin. It does not mean that mankind does not exercise some restraint over evil. This does not mean that every person is as bad as they possibly can be. This does not mean that from a human perspective people cannot do good things. It does mean that, bottom line, all are corrupt in their innermost being.

1. Edwards, "The Justice of God in the Damnation of Sinners, " 124–25.

I once heard an atheist debating a Christian about the existence of God. The atheist was relating that he and his atheist friends did good things. But, in an absolute sense, God is the final judge of whether those things were good things. Since they were not done for the glory of God (it is hard to imagine that an atheist would be doing something for the glory of God), those things done were not good in an absolute sense. (I will not even get into the dilemma an atheist puts himself in when he speaks of actions being good in some absolute sense!) However, I think it is safe to say that the atheist liked the good things he was doing. What I am saying is that the unregenerate do what they like and want to do. And what they like and want to do is sin before a holy God. So the bottom line here is that at the center of one's self-glory is a heart that only sins.

THE BELIEVER'S NEW HEART

So it makes sense that the solution to our self-glorying must be some kind of change of heart (literally, a changing of our inner nature!). That is exactly what God does. In fact, when we speak of breaking the power of self-glory, I want to be clear that it is God who does the breaking! He does this by giving lost and hopeless sinners a new heart that brings with it a real faith in Christ that, in turn, brings with it a changed life. These three elements are inextricably linked together. Through the gospel, God makes us alive toward God. This is technically called regeneration. We need regeneration because our natural disposition is not toward God but away from him. This is what Jesus meant when he said, "Unless one is born again, he cannot see the kingdom of God" (John

3:3). With this new heart, given to us by grace and through the means of the gospel message, we embrace Jesus Christ and his salvation by faith. We are then justified. Justification is the doctrine that God, on the basis of what Christ has done on our behalf, forgives our sins and declares us righteous (Romans 3:21–22). In Justification, Christ's righteousness is imputed to us ("to impute" means "to put to one's account on the basis of what someone else has done"). Our sin is placed upon Christ. It is quite an exchange—his perfect life for our sinful one! We are justified through the agency of faith but on the basis of Christ's work. Our faith comes out of our new heart. In the logical order of salvation, the new heart comes first, thus we are enabled to believe (1 John 5:1). In real life, they occur together—the new heart being a heart that believes. There is no such thing, practically speaking, as someone who has been regenerated who does not believe. Neither is there such a thing as someone who has believed who has not first been regenerated. The life of regeneration is the life of faith in Christ. Of course, this is all by God's grace and for his glory. Now we are ready to see that with this new heart come new affections, feelings, and desires.

THE CROSS AND THE BELIEVER'S OWN CRUCIFIXION

Here is where we must take a closer look at Christ's work on the cross. Christians, for the most part, are aware that Jesus Christ died for them. They must also be aware that they died with him! Here is a useful saying for every believer: "he died for us; we died with him." Galatians 5:24 makes clear the manner in which we were crucified with Christ:

"And those *who are* Christ's have crucified the flesh with its passions and desires." Notice what has been crucified. What a glorious truth! The old affections, lusts, desires, passions—they have been put to death in the reality of Christ's cross. Now, here comes the center of this important truth. The believer's regenerate heart has now been freed to love God! The power of self-glory has been definitively broken. We may say with Paul, "I have been crucified with Christ; it is no longer I who live, but Christ lives in me; and the *life* which I now live in the flesh I live by faith in the Son of God, who loved me and gave himself for me" (Galatians 2:20). Now, we can pursue what is commanded in Philippians 4:4: "Rejoice in the Lord always. Again I will say, rejoice!" Now, we can recognize that in God there is joy. He gives us joy in himself not in self-glorifying and lustful pleasures. We must no longer simply use God to make much of ourselves but we must make much of him and delight in him. Joy in God becomes a driving force in our lives. Living out the Christian life is not drudgery or merely a duty. It is a blessed experience. The power of self-glory has been broken in the cross! This is good news indeed. With a new heart disposed to desire God, we can now pursue the joy that we were made for—joy in God himself!

GOD'S GLORY AND OUR HAPPINESS MEET IN JESUS CHRIST

Here is more really great news. The absolute truth is that in the ultimate sense just as God desires his children to glorify him, he desires his children to be happy. His glory and our happiness are not at odds. They meet together in

Jesus Christ. When we speak about breaking the power of self-glory, we are not saying that we become beings devoid of self-interest. We are simply recognizing that it is in our best interest to glorify God not us. We were designed to delight in something outside of ourselves. Our sinful nature takes our natural self-interest and self-love to a sinful and ungodly realm. In this sinful self-centeredness, we want the glory that is rightfully God's alone. It is this sinfulness that is broken in the cross. We begin to see God's greatness, perfection, majesty, beauty, and holiness. Desires for God that were not present before become real.

THEN HOW COME I STILL HAVE PROBLEMS

If the power of self-glory has been broken, if my old affections, lusts, desires, and passions have all been put to death, then why do I still sin? Why is this not as easy as it sounds? In fact, why is it still sometimes very difficult? These are certainly relevant questions. The proper theological answer, I believe, lies in a simple fact. God ordained this reality to be worked out progressively over time. Although the cross provides the decisive blow to the old desires, the transformation is worked out during our lifetime as a believer. Ultimate victory is certain. Sin's power has been definitively broken. Sin's reign in our hearts has been dethroned. Nonetheless, the actual transformation is done over the course of real time. All believers know the reality of the struggle as we are changed over time. We simply note here that this transformation requires our cooperation. We will discuss our part later in the book. For now, it is important for you to keep in mind that although we can properly speak of "our part," this transformation is still all of grace. God, in fact, provides all the means through which he brings about this radical transformation. Let me say something now about one of the very important means through which God works. This dynamic transformation involves the Spirit of God working in us as we behold the glory of Jesus Christ. It is clearly stated in 2 Corinthians 3:18: "But we all, with unveiled face, beholding as in a mirror the glory of the Lord, are being transformed into the same image from glory to glory, just as by the Spirit of the Lord." As we see God revealed in the person and work of Jesus Christ through the "mirror" of Scripture, we are brought from one level of glory to another (one stage of spiritual life to another) by the Holy Spirit. We must continually see Christ as he is unfolded in the pages of Scripture. Then, more and more, our hearts will be drawn closer and closer to him. He will become, more and more, the object of our joy. In the following chapter, we will look at this progressive growth process.

7

Growing in the Grace of Glorifying God

GOD IS glorious and desires to be known for his glory. Believers have been given a new nature that desires to glorify God. Hopefully these truths have been established in your heart through God's Word and by his Spirit. Yet, as we saw in the previous chapter, there is a progressive nature to our transformation. So as we look now at a believer's growth, let's be sure to understand that the goal is always to glorify God. Some Christians would say that the goal of a believer is to become Christlike. This is absolutely true (Romans 8:29). God has sovereignly determined that we be transformed over time into the image of Jesus Christ. However, we must put this concept into its proper perspective. First of all, this does not mean that we become like God. We are not growing into omnipotence or omniscience. We can never be eternal beings for we came into existence in real time. Only God is God. So God's goal of Christlikeness for our lives does not mean we become a god ourselves! Secondly, we must consider what characteristics of Christ God does desire us to imitate. We ought to seek to become like Christ in many areas: love, compassion, wisdom, patience, obedience to the Father, etc. However, our focus here is on one area that is extremely significant and most often neglected. Jesus Christ lives for the glory of his Father! Now, conversely, the Father delights in glorifying the Son, but that is not what we are dealing with in our discussion. In our seeking to be Christlike, it only makes sense that we should seek to be like Christ in the area that is actually our main purpose of existence—living for the glory of God. Jesus is our supreme example! That is what we see in Christ's earthly life, in his death on the cross, and even in his exaltation. Philippians 2:9–11 says, "Therefore God also has highly exalted him and given him the name which is above every name, that at the name of Jesus every knee should bow, of those in heaven, and of those on earth, and of those under the earth, and *that* every tongue should confess that Jesus Christ *is* Lord, to the glory of God the Father." Notice the very last phrase—"to the glory of God the Father"! Whatever Christ does glorifies his Father because he is always in complete submission and union with his Father. His desire is to only and always please his Father (John 8:29). We are most like Christ when we are seeking to glorify God alone. It is when our hearts and minds desire that the Father be exalted, when we delight in praising God, when we want his name to be magnified, when he is our supreme treasure. So when I say that our spiritual growth is for the goal of making much of God, for glorifying him, I am not speaking against the goal of Christlikeness. I am expressing that ultimately our Christlikeness is for the purpose of glorifying God! So we will now examine spiritual growth with the goal of God's glory in mind.

A BASIC UNDERSTANDING OF PROGRESSIVE
SANCTIFICATION

Progressive Sanctification is the theological term for this actual transformation we have been talking about. It can be defined as a continual work of God that moves a believer more and more away from sinfulness and toward actively glorifying God in one's heart and one's life. So we are talking here about actual changes. For example, our thoughts are becoming more and more God-centered. When I was younger, I was a great daydreamer. I remember sitting in high school classes with my mind a million miles away. Sometimes I was flying down the ice like Bobby Orr. Other times I was on stage playing my guitar and singing while screaming fans were shouting out my name. No wonder my grades were not exactly stellar! Hey, does that sound a little self-glorifying? It certainly was (not to mention just a bit foolish!). We can think in a self-glorifying way. We can think in a God glorifying way. The important question for me now as a believer is: "Where is my mind these days?" As I grow spiritually, it will be more and more on the things of God. Believers are supposed to have great thoughts about God! How about our deeds—what are we actually doing? Again, Progressive Sanctification means that my deeds are changing. My life is spent, more and more, doing God-glorifying good works. In a future chapter, we will specifically talk about how one's good works can glorify God. For now, I am merely saying that in sanctification we are speaking about actual change—spiritual growth. For brevity's sake, allow me to list some foundational truths that go along with Progressive Sanctification.

1. There is a sense in Scripture in which sanctification is seen as a status conferred upon us by God based upon Christ's merits. In other words, there is a sense in which we have already been, once for all time, set apart (sanctified) from sin unto God. Hebrews 10:10 expresses this truth so well: "By that will we have been sanctified through the offering of the body of Jesus Christ once *for all.*" This is our blessed position in Christ. Nothing can now separate us from his love (Romans 8:35). Nothing can stop his work to bring us to full redemption (Philippians 1:6). This kind of sanctification is so wonderful, yet it is to be distinguished from Progressive Sanctification.

2. Progressive Sanctification deals with the fact that believers have not yet arrived in terms of practical holiness. We are all far, very far, from it. Therefore holiness must be pursued. Growth should be happening. All with the ultimate goal of God's glory in focus (1 Peter 2:2; 2 Peter 3:18).

3. Progress continues throughout the life of a believer. Perfection does not come completely until the Lord returns and changes us into our final state (Philippians 3:20–21; 1 John 3:2). It is in this final state that we know God's glory by sight and not merely by faith. Glorifying God does not stop then. It is our eternal focus. There will be a fullness of joy as we will experience God's great glory forever.

4. This sanctification is a work of God's grace. It is God growing us, God conforming us. However, we cooperate actively not passively. We are to be focused on this growth because we desire to increasingly and very actively make much of God as we live in the midst of a fallen world that makes much of man (Romans 6:11; 2 Corinthians 7:1).

5. All self-glorying activity moves us away from spiritual growth. We must constantly remind ourselves that we are crucified with Christ. We never move away from a cross-centered, gospel-centered life. We actually grow deeper in it (Galatians 2:20).

These foundational facts help us in our movement toward the goal. In evangelical circles, there have been some different *systems* that have come about in an effort to promote sanctification. Not all of these systems are actually Biblical. We will talk about two that are definitely false and do not promote real spiritual and God-glorifying growth. These two *systems* are known as *legalism* and *license*. I am calling them systems, but they are of the informal type. This means that no church or theologian has actually written a theological philosophy of legalism or license to be practiced by the church. These systems vary widely as to how they are practiced. Some people mingle parts of them together. Most systems of legalism or license are impure mixtures of both! For purposes of our understanding of these systems, I will treat them separately and highlight their errors. Then we will look at a valid system called *liberty*. Properly understood, this system is Biblical and will help you grow in the grace of glorifying God!

LEGALISM

Back in the second chapter of this book, we spoke of growing by being nourished with gospel truth not with rules or *how to* messages. This is truly foundational to growing spiritually in such a way that God is glorified. When you strip legalism of all of its pseudo-spirituality, it is simply a religion of human accomplishment undergirded by man's pride. Behind legalism is the idea that one either merits salvation by one's own works or that one grows spiritually by one's own works. These works amount to a set of rules and regulations thought to carry with them a spirituality for those who obey. Even if the *rules* are presented to us in a *how to* fashion, we are still called upon to perform. The problem is that we cannot perform apart from God's grace. God is not interested in self-performance for self-performance glorifies one's self! We are not in some sort of spiritual game with Jesus Christ on the sidelines shouting instructions to us and saying, "You can do it." We do not need to hear preaching that says, "Try harder, you can do it!" We need to hear the truth about salvation. From start to finish, it is God's work! Many times, in legalistic systems, the rules and regulations are usually dictated by someone in authority according to this leader's own ideas. In other words, the group follows his rules. They are not allowed to think for themselves. In some cases, this authority figure is "the man of God" people believe they have been placed under and they dare not question his authority. Also, the focus of many legalistic systems is external. It is about how one looks and not about one's heart. In some cases, the error of legalism is this: the conversion part of salvation is seen as a work of God's grace; the rest of salvation is seen as the work of the individual. A continuous work of grace is just not understood. Here is the great danger of legalism: the legalist misplaces Christian joy—he sees joy in himself as he performs! He presents his own works before God thinking that God will be pleased. He is like the Pharisee Jesus spoke about in Luke 18:9–12. He loved his own works and despised those deemed less spiritual. The Pharisee in Christ's parable boasted about what he brought to the table in terms of his spiritual life. The Pharisee looked down on the tax collector who was also praying in the temple. However, Jesus said that the tax collector went home justified. The tax collector realized his need for God's mercy. He recognized who he really was. The Pharisee did not go away justified. He went away in his own self-glory. Legalism is a system that kills real spirituality because it promotes self-glory not God's glory.

LICENSE

Behind this system is the idea that, since a believer is under grace and not under the law, sin isn't really that important any more. What is most important is that we love one another. God doesn't mind one's sins any more because he has forgiven them. Those who practice this system understand the demands of the law are too great. They understand that God has poured his grace upon believers. What they do not see is that Christ has demands as well. Perhaps *demands* is not the right word because of its harsh connotations. However, it is clear. Jesus has expectations for those who follow him. The New Testament is full of commands. Those commands are not all that simple to follow. For example: we are to love one another as Christ loved us; we are to pray without ceasing; we are to perfecting holiness in the fear of God. Those who practice license (also called antinomianism, which means "without law"), fail to see these commands, and also fail to see that God's grace is actively working in our lives enabling us to follow Christ. In other words, it is possible to seek to follow Christ in humble obedience without self-performance. We follow by grace. So underlying antinomianism is a false understanding of grace. We do not continue in sin that grace might abound (Romans 6:1)! Now the truth is that I do not know any believers who would openly ascribe to this system. What I do see are those who basically abuse the concept of grace. They seem to think that God's grace says: "Don't worry so much about personal holiness, God isn't that concerned. He doesn't really mind sin anymore." God, however, is concerned. He is concerned that our affections and will are toward him. That we are not running around fulfilling the desires of our sinful flesh, but that we are living for his glory (1 Peter 2:11). Let me close out this section on the system of license by describing how it seems to work out in practice. In this way of thinking, truth is seen as very flexible and of secondary importance. It seems as though many believers do not want to be bothered with doctrine while they are following Christ! Many focus on a therapeutically-driven lifestyle. God is used to affirm one's value. The ultimate goal is to feel good about oneself. The cross itself is used to validate one's self worth, after all, God died for me. I must be worth it. I hope you see that this turns grace on its head. The fact that Christ died for sinners, magnifies his greatness not ours! Many simply pursue their own natural affections and desires much like an unsaved person. The tragedy is that these folks are a poor example for others in the church, and are a horrible testimony to the world. Legalism and License are not valid systems to follow for real spiritual growth for God's glory. Let's look at a system that is valid.

LIBERTY

Again, these systems are not formal. However they are real. Believers who understand real Christian liberty grow spiritually because when real liberty is practiced, one finds the work of the Spirit of God (2 Corinthians 3:17). It is the Holy Sprit's work to show us the glory of God and to change us into Christlikeness (2 Corinthians 3:18). Liberty is sometimes abused and what is actually practiced in its name is license. The real system of liberty is what we want to now examine. In liberty, the believer understands that he has been liberated from the bondage of sin which was his pre-salvation condition (Ephesians 2:3; John 8:32, 36; Galatians 5:24). Behind this system, one understands God's grace as that which is continually working. Grace is seen as an active and enabling force (1 Corinthians 15:10; 2 Corinthians 12:9). Thus true liberty means that one is free to pursue living for the glory of God by grace and through the work of the indwelling Holy Spirit. Having been changed internally in regeneration, one's desire for God can be pursued. In practicing liberty, believers do not ignore the moral and spiritual laws of God. They understand that through God's grace and the Holy Spirit's work, a life of holiness for God's glory is being produced according to God's perfect standards and not against them (Romans 8:4). Believers must understand that this spiritual growth does not happen in a vacuum. God's grace and his Spirit work through means. For the rest of this chapter, let's briefly look at some of the means that God uses under this system of liberty to grow us in the grace of glorifying God.

THE FEAR OF THE LORD

As I begin to write this, I already *fear* (no pun intended) that this expression will not be well received. That's really a shame, because proper fear of God is an essential element in our sanctification. In fact it is the necessary beginning point! Proverbs 1:7 states, "The fear of the LORD *is* the beginning of knowledge, *But* fools despise wisdom and instruction." Proverbs 9:10 states a similar thought: "The fear of the LORD *is* the beginning of wisdom, And the knowledge of the Holy One *is* understanding." We must not, however, think of fearing God in isolation, as if it stands apart from love or grace. It is an integral part of loving God. It is part of God's grace working in our hearts. In his book *Grow In Grace*, Sinclair Ferguson makes the distinction between *servile* fear and *filial* fear. He describes servile fear as "a fear which a slave would feel toward a harsh and unyielding master"[1] and filial fear as "the loving fear which a child feels toward his father."[2] Servile fear is that terrifying fear that does not cause love and respect. It certainly does not help us love God. It produces just the opposite reaction. If I were to be kidnapped at gunpoint, I would surely fear my kidnappers. I do not think I would describe my feelings toward them as very loving! When God changes a person's heart, things become much different. Terror is banished from the genuine believer's heart. I John 4:18 states, "There is no fear in love; but perfect love casts out fear, because fear involves torment. But he who fears has not been made perfect in love." Filial fear (*filial* is from the Latin *filius* meaning "a

1. Ferguson, *Grow in Grace*, 28.
2. Ibid., 28.

son") is one of reverence, respect, awe, pleasure, and joy. It is that element that fills our heart when we contemplate God in his fullness. It actually moves us to desire him (Psalm 5:7; 112:1; 128:1, 2) Fearing God is not to be thought of as an Old Testament concept that has been done away with in the New Testament because of grace. In fact, fearing God is practiced by grace! Hebrews 12:28 states, "Therefore, since we are receiving a kingdom which cannot be shaken, let us have grace, by which we may serve God acceptably with reverence and godly fear." God graciously places in our hearts a proper view of him, a view of him that causes us to be in awe and respect him supremely.

How does the fear of God relate to our growth? Put negatively, proper fear causes us not to ignore, avoid, or make light of God's purpose for us to live for his glory. Put positively, proper fear causes us to rightly make much of God and pursue his will for our lives (Ecclesiastes 12:3). Living in the fear of God moves us to seek his holiness in our lives, based on the promise that he is our God and we are his children (II Corinthians 7:1). This filial respect and awe of God removes human fears that can hinder our spiritual progress. It moves us to diligently cooperate with God's Spirit in our growth (Philippians 2:12–13).

LONGING

This means of growth is simple. Because of God's grace and out of our new nature, believers desire to grow from the very depths of their soul (Psalm 63:1–3; Isaiah 26:8–9). I like the way this is expressed in 1 Peter 2:2–3: "As newborn babes, desire the pure milk of the word, that you may grow thereby, if indeed you have tasted that the Lord *is* gracious." Notice why one would desire the Word of God? It is because one has tasted the Lord's graciousness. If we have truly experienced a changed heart and understood the realities of what Jesus has done for us, Peter's point is that we will want to know more! The word *tasted* does not mean a casual sampling. It means that we have experienced personally and enjoyed the experience of God's grace. When this happens, we want to know God. We want to know more about his excellent qualities. We want to know more about how we can exalt him. I am not saying that we will not struggle. I am not saying that there will not be a battle sometimes internally. I am not saying that this longing may, at times, be very weak indeed. But, praise God, it is there in the heart of a believer. Precisely because he has tasted God's grace in salvation, our hearts long to know God.

LEARNING

The longing spoken of above directs us to God's Word that we might know and understand more and more about our glorious God. The more we understand, the more glorious we recognize God is. The more glorious we recognize God is, the more able we are to express this in our words and deeds! That is why Paul prayed a great deal for believers to grow in their understanding. He desired that God would open their eyes more and more to the glories of their salvation (Ephesians 1:18–19). This is why it is important that we understand that the whole Bible focuses on Jesus Christ. We must not look at the Bible as an interesting academic or history book. We must seek Jesus Christ. It is a book about him. It is a gospel book. It is a book about the history of redemption planned by God and worked out over thousands of years of God's working through history. Hebrews 13:9 tells us that the heart of a believer must be "established by grace." This means that we, as God's sheep, must be fed gospel food that nourishes our souls. We must seek to understand the gospel from all Biblical angles. We must see its many awesome doctrines. We must let God's grace saturate our souls. We must be learning the Word that we may grow in the grace of living for the glory of God.

SPIRITUAL DISCIPLINES

Discipline is another word that I fear will be a turn-off. But it must not be, for the spiritual disciplines are one of the most important means God uses through which he grows us. We talked about learning. This does not happen by chance. One of the spiritual disciplines is that we spend regular time in God's Word. We must read it, study it, and meditate upon it. This is hard work. We must also be good hearers of the Word as it is preached. God has ordained certain men to be spiritual leaders whose job it is to feed his flock. As these men teach and preach God's Word, it is the believer's responsibility to pay very close attention. There are many other spiritual disciplines. Let's think of one more—prayer. Through earnest prayer we draw close to God. We ask for more *want to*. We worship and praise. Again, earnest prayer is not easy. It is meant to be a regular exercise in our spiritual lives. Rather than go on and on about spiritual disciplines (because I really do mean for all this to be brief), let me make really the main point here. Spiritual disciplines are the spiritual exercises God has designed for our progress in spiritual life. Consider 1 Timothy 4:7: "But reject profane and old wives' fables, and exercise yourself toward godliness." Notice the word *exercise*. It translates the Greek word *gumnazo*. Our English words *gymnastics* and *gymnasium* are derived from this word. It speaks here of vigorous spiritual exercise. That's why we call these spiritual disciplines. They will not be easy to do. They require, well, discipline! Yet they are a part of God's grace. He gives us the strength. Christ is our great example. He models these for us (Mark 1:35). These must not be reduced to mindless, heartless, spiritual drudgery. We must pursue these disciplines with mind and heart fully engaged. They must be seen as gracious means to a God-glorifying life.

THE CHURCH

The last in this list of means through which God grows us is the local church. The local church isn't actually a church building or even a place to meet. It isn't primarily an organization. It is a manifestation of the body of Christ at a local level. Among other things, it is to be recognized as a vital part of a believer's means of growing. God has designed the church body to function as a means of growth for individual believers. In other words, spiritual growth ought to be done in the context of a church body. Going to church is not a spectator event. We are to participate in worship, praise, learning, praying, giving, and helping one another to grow. Christians are to connect with one another in their life's experiences with the goal of building up one another in the faith (1 Corinthians 12:26; 14:12). We are to continually exhort one another to maintain steadfastness. This exhortation includes encouragement, comfort, instruction, correction, and admonition (Hebrews 3:13; 10:25). Serious sinful behavior is to be confronted within the church body (Galatians 6:1). More mature believers are to set an example for the others in the body (Titus 2:7). The local church ought to be all of the above and more. There is no such thing, practically speaking, of a spiritually-minded believer living his Christian life without participation in a local assembly. Church is a vital part of spiritual life and growth.

WRAPPING IT UP

Many believers understand that spiritual growth is supposed to be happening. They even understand at least some of how it happens. This chapter certainly has not said all that there is to say. What I do want you to understand is where spiritual growth fits into a life lived for the glory of God. I hope you see its vital connection. God is transforming us in order that we can know him more fully. This is so that we can exalt him all the more! Our goal is always to glorify God. Our goal is always to see this as a great joy. Our goal is to recognize that he alone is worthy. May we be growing in grace toward this for it is our purpose for existence!

8

Five Huge Substitutions

Iɴ ᴛʜɪs chapter we are going to look at some lifestyles that will not do if our purpose of existence is to actively live for the glory of God. I have used this word *actively* before and I want to take just a moment to explain what I mean by it. By *actively living for the glory of God*, I mean that God will ultimately be glorified in all things. When all is finally revealed, we will see that this world and all that happened were the outworking of a perfect plan. Every detail has been designed for God to receive glory. I say this, because of two main truths. First, God is sovereign in every detail of this world. I am not going to delve into this at any great length because it is simply too profound a subject and would certainly require a lot more writing (Not to mention that many others have done a far better job explaining this than I would be able to). What I will say is this: the Bible teaches that there is a God who is sovereign over all things. This means bad things and good things, right things and wrong things, health and suffering, life and death. God is in control; he ordains it all. This is what the Scriptures teach. Let me just put a few verses in front of you to contemplate.

Deuteronomy 32:39 Now see that I, *even* I, *am* he, And *there is* no God besides Me; I kill and I make alive; I wound and I heal; Nor *is there any* who can deliver from My hand.

Psalm 115:3 But our God *is* in heaven; he does whatever he pleases.

Proverbs 16:33 The lot is cast into the lap, But its every decision *is* from the LORD.

Isaiah 45:6-7 That they may know from the rising of the sun to its setting That *there is* none besides Me. I *am* the LORD, and *there is* no other; I form the light and create darkness, I make peace and create calamity; I, the LORD, do all these *things.'*

Acts 2:23 "him, being delivered by the determined purpose and foreknowledge of God, you have taken by lawless hands, have crucified, and put to death."

Acts 4:27-28 "For truly against Your holy Servant Jesus, whom You anointed, both Herod and Pontius Pilate, with the Gentiles and the people of Israel, were gathered together to do whatever Your hand and Your purpose determined before to be done."

Ephesians 1:11 In him also we have obtained an inheritance, being predestined according to the purpose of him who works all things according to the counsel of his will.

Now, all this must not be understood to say that God is evil. He absolutely is not! His ordination of all things does not mean that all the evil things that he allows flow out of his pure and holy nature. They do not. Nonetheless, he permits them to come into existence with absolute control. He could have stopped every single evil to date. He could refuse any future evil to happen. He is sovereign. That is the first truth. The second is that God is perfect. Every thing that he does is perfect. He makes no mistakes. Do you see the implication? Nothing that *has* happened has been an accident or a mistake. Nothing that *will* happen has been an accident or mistake. In the end, we will see all things coming together for God's glory. Another way of saying this is that God has designed the universe to maximize his glory. If there were a better way to do this, he would have done it that way! So, though the wicked certainly do not *actively* glorify God, in the end, God will be glorified in their judgment, as he will also be glorified in the grace and mercy that he showed to the saved. These are truly remarkable statements that our finite minds can grasp only in part. My point is that no one can escape the glory of God. All things have been created by him and for him! That is why I use the word *active* in terms of a believer's living for the glory of God. God desires us to glorify him on purpose! We live for God's glory with our whole mind, and strength, and emotions. We live for God's glory by his grace. But it is an active kind of living. We do it on purpose. We want to do it. We desire God to be known for his glory.

The point of this chapter is that some who profess to be Christians do not actively pursue God's glory. They have substituted other lifestyles rather than take up, by God's grace, the life of God-centeredness. Those redeemed are to "be to the praise of his glory" (Ephesians 1:12). This means that believers have a different center to their lives than the unregenerate. In a very real way, Jesus Christ is "our life" (Colossians 3:4). Christians love him (1 Corinthians 16:22), desire to know him more intimately (Philippians 3:10), and look forward to abundant rejoicing in his presence someday (1 Peter 4:13; Psalm 16:11). To glorify God is to renounce self-glory. To glorify self is to renounce God's glory. All believers must have God's glory in view, otherwise they really dishonor God (1 Corinthians 1:29). Nothing must be substituted for God-centered Christianity. It almost seems foolish to have to make such a statement. But so many ways of living have been substituted for a lifestyle that is God-glorifying. Here are five that I have seen in the contemporary church. I point these out because we all struggle with these to some extent. I know that I certainly have. So, as you examine these, my prayer is that they will help you identify parts of your life that result in God not being at the center.

THE PRAGMATIC-MATERIAL LIFE

This lifestyle is the "whatever works for me" lifestyle. Instead of an active pursuit of God's glory, the professing Christian strives for the very same things that the world strives for. Taking his cue from the world's definition of success, the believer proceeds to strive for this man-made success. To accomplish this, he uses whatever works. He may strive for money, power, prestige, a comfortable life, lots of stuff. This pragmatism can even be lived out in one's ministry. The believer works hard to build a big church, have authority over large amounts of people, prestige among his peers, and the acclaim of his audience. Theology is cast off and whatever works is the primary focus. The church continually looks for the latest trendy programs to climb to new levels of success. Success is measured much like the world measures it—finances, health, popularity, prominence, power, etc. The idea is to use whatever works to ultimately glorify self (and, of course, to help promote the Kingdom). Whether in secular pursuits or in ministry, the goal is, in the end, self-glory. This lifestyle is many times driven by pride and fueled by envy (Philippians 2:3; Galatians 5:26; James 3:14). I am not saying, of course, that hard work or being practical is wrong. I am talking about an underlying philosophy of pragmatism that is being used to promote man-made goals. In *Christless Christianity*, Michael Horton speaks of "the transcendent God of majesty and holiness" being reduced to "a casual familiarity" and religion being "privatized into a kind of therapeutic usefulness . . . We recognize this pragmatic orientation in the 'how to' literature that lines the shelves of Christian bookstores and pastors' studies."[1] Many want to know how to succeed in their own self-centered pursuits and the church has unfortunately responded by giving the *customer* what he wants. Some in the church seem to be focused on whatever works to get them ahead rather than on glorifying God. This is a huge sin. We have God-ordained means that we might strive for the ultimate God-ordained goal—living for the glory of God. As one studies the life of Christ, one realizes that Jesus apparently did not see the need to use church-growth techniques in his ministry. Although he did draw some large crowds, he also drove them away with his preaching and teaching of the truth. The sixth chapter of John's gospel begins with a very large crowd following Jesus. After some very serious teaching, it ends with many walking away from him and only a handful of disciples left. When all is said and done it

1. Horton, *Christless Christianity*, 52, 53.

comes down to this: we must live through the God-ordained means that he has provided; we must reject philosophies that ignore these means whether they seem to work or not. We must certainly have our hearts toward the things of God and not on this sinful world (Matthew 6:19–21).

THE SELF-ESTEEM FOCUSED LIFE

This way of living is based on secular philosophies that are therapeutically-driven not theologically driven. I have noticed that much of the contemporary church's reading material is written by psychologists not pastors with sound theological understanding. In this self-esteem focused life, God is used to affirm our value and ultimately *self* is worshipped. The goal is to feel good about oneself (apart from actually being good). The problem of course is that, in reality, there is no one who is actually good (Romans 3:10–18). The only real way to be seen in God's eyes as good is to have Christ's righteousness placed upon oneself. It is from this position that one may then grow in grace and become more like Christ. This is all by grace and all for God's glory. Biblically, it would be much better if believers would understand the depth of their sinfulness and rely solely on the grace of God. It would not hurt us to cry out like Job "Behold, I am vile" (Job 40:4). Like Paul, we should all consider ourselves the chiefest of sinners (1 Timothy 1:15). This would allow us to magnify God's grace and live for his glory. Instead, God is used to promote our self-glory. Believers focus on God's gifts but ignore his person. They are thankful for the things they get from God but do not pursue a vision of his character for his exaltation. Again, we want God to be the source of our joy but not the object of it. None of this is to deny that all men have a natural and normal self-interest. In this normal and natural self-interest, believers must know that it is in their best interest for God to be glorified not self. The self-esteem focused life flows from self-interest that has been captured by the corruption of indwelling sinfulness. Thus, the unregenerate heart's passion is for self-exaltation. If God can help one with this kind of self-glory, then fine. So goes the thinking of the self-esteem focused *Christian*. In our culture, our young people are being reared on self-esteem philosophy. This has spilled over into Christian families in large number. We have been blinded by our sin-based desire for self-glory. Parents believe that to love their children means helping their children to feel good about themselves, love themselves, and make much about themselves. Christians need to understand that we love people by helping them know and exalt Jesus Christ. We love our children by giving them a vision of the glory of God through teaching and example. The great need in Christian homes is Christian parents who have a passionate desire to glorify God. The lifestyle that focuses on self-esteem is a poor substitute indeed for a life that is lived to actively glorify God.

THE "FUZZY" TRUTH LIFE

In this way of living, the professing Christian begins to see truth as very flexible and of secondary importance. The Scriptures cease in their role of unfolding to believers the great truths of redemption in the very specific doctrines of God's grace. The believer's life is not oriented by God's Word so much as it is oriented by various experiences and vague notions of love. The believer does not see the link between truth and worship, between doctrine and practice. Passages of Scripture eventually get used and abused. God is not worshipped in truth (John 4:24); he is changed into whatever one wants him to be. After all, what's most important is that we love him and each other. There is a failure to see that God must be glorified for who he is. There is a failure to see that he has revealed to us who he is in his Word. Sound doctrine and sound Christian living go hand in hand. Truth sanctifies and nurtures (John 17:17; 1 Peter 2:3). Believers must grow in grace and knowledge as well (2 Peter 3:18). How great is the need to return to the God-ordained means of genuine gospel preaching and teaching. We have already discussed the inadequacy of *how to* messages that leave off the gospel and see God as someone who offers us the best of advice. We need pastors who will take seriously the duty of the study of God's Word. They need to see the weightiness of their duty to feed God's flock. We need congregations to see the great importance of the proper hearing of the Word of God. We need God's truth to rise up to the place that it belongs in local churches. We need believers who will seek out God's truths with diligence recognizing his truth as the treasure that it surely is!

THE BUSY RELIGIOUS WORKS LIFE

This is the life of self-glorifying works; the life of earning one's salvation or earning one's sanctification. It is a life that denies the continuous work of grace. Denying grace is not glorifying to God. This life moves further and further away from the cross and relies more and more on self-performance. One is busy with doing but not with growing in grace. Personal holiness is measured by the amount of service more than the heart and character of the individual. It goes hand in hand with the lack of understanding today of the need for any kind of perseverance in the faith (remember the three tenses of salvation from chapter 1). There is the common perception among professing evangelicals that one is saved by grace, and then, performs works for God to earn favor and rewards. God is not seen as the real reward of our persevering faith. Thus, believers perform for God. The joy they have is misplaced. It is not in Christ but in one's own performance. I know I have already discussed this, but it is so important to understand. Here is the real problem: one may be busy serving God while at the same time not really knowing God. Yet, the New Testament is clear that the believer is to understand that it is only because of Christ that he can do anything (John 15:5). All boasting must be firmly anchored in the cross (Galatians 6:14). Ministry must all be done in God's power for his glory. Peter puts it this way, "If anyone speaks, *let him speak* as the oracles of God. If anyone ministers, *let him do it* as with the ability which God supplies, that in all things God may be glorified through Jesus Christ, to whom belong the glory and the dominion forever and ever. Amen" (1 Peter 4:11). Notice that all ability comes from God. We are not busy helping him out. He is gracious in using us as a means through which he works. Good works can glorify God, but only when they are properly understood (more on that later). When we see these works as coming from our own capable hands, we are in big trouble spiritually. This life is not an acceptable substitute for living for God's glory alone.

THE DIFFERENT AIMS
AND TIMEFRAMES LIFE

I have encountered many believers who seem to operate under this philosophy. These professing Christians believe that the aim now is duty and later, in heaven, delight. We must serve God now, enjoy him later. So the Christian life is the hard life of discipline, duty, work, and suffering. Joy is an option. Sometimes joy is present but not most of the time. This kind of thinking often places a great emphasis on God's needing us. I have actually heard believers say, "I don't know what this church would do without me!" They have no joy in service, but they have a great need to work and feel important. Again, duty now, delight later. The problem with this thinking is that a false dichotomy is created. It does not have to be one or the other. In fact, these two aims must converge! Glorifying God and enjoying him co-exist. Indeed, they must co-exist. Your works do not honor God if there is no joy accompanying them. God is not exalted if we essentially say: "I am doing this for you but I don't really like it." When we see God's worth, when he is our treasure, when he is the object of our joy, we will gladly serve (Psalm 100:2). This is not to say service for his Kingdom is easy. Not at all. He has already assured us that it will not be so (John 15:18–19; 16:33). But because of the hope that is set before us, we run the race with patience . . .and also with joy! This is not heaven. However, a life absent of joy does not glorify God.

CONCLUSION:
WE MUST BE GOD-CENTERED

Do not substitute these things for a God-Centered life. God created us to be satisfied in him alone. We have been made in such a way that only something outside of ourselves will bring us true joy. That "something" is actually God. Believers are commanded to be God-Centered. We are commanded to glorify God in everything we do (1 Corinthians 10:31). These wonderful thoughts ought to drive us continually to our knees in prayer seeking more grace. We must ask God to grant us the reality of the cross. In the cross, God has broken the power of self-glory. We must humbly come before him for the help and grace we need that we may exalt him. We must actively glorify our worthy God. In the next chapter, we will see one very important way to avoid falling prey to these substitute lifestyles. It is by staying focused on the cross of Jesus Christ.

9

· Cross-Centeredness

IN GALATIANS 6:14, Paul proclaims, "But God forbid that I should boast except in the cross of our Lord Jesus Christ, by whom the world has been crucified to me, and I to the world." Martyn Lloyd-Jones writes in his book *The Cross*, which is based on this verse in Galatians, "You cannot remain neutral in the presence of the cross. It has always divided mankind and it still does. And what the Apostle says is that there are ultimately only two positions with respect to it. The cross of our Lord Jesus Christ is either an offense to us or else it is the thing above everything else in which we glory."[1] We have seen that there are some substitute lifestyles that can replace living actively for the glory of God. To avoid a serious detour from God-centeredness, a believer in Jesus Christ must be cross-centered. It is through the cross that all the blessings of the Christian life come to us. Apart from the gospel, we would be without hope—utterly lost. I have seen many believers and many churches where it seems that the real-life theology (what is practiced) is that the cross is simply for evangelistic purposes. Once someone is "saved" they must move on. Early in my Christian life, I was very familiar with many churches whose philosophy was "win

1. Lloyd-Jones, *The Cross*, 41.

them, wet them, work them." People were, in a very real sense, moved quickly away from the cross. The goal, after a profession of faith, was mainly to serve. The truth is that believers must never move away from the cross. We grow deeper in the depths of its wisdom and power. We must not move away. We can only glorify God through the cross of Jesus Christ. His accomplishments on our behalf ought to cause us to exalt God alone. Our redemption through Christ's cross was the purposeful design of the Father, was executed perfectly by the Son, and is effectively applied to our hearts by the Holy Spirit. Our tri-une God is glorified in a cross-centered life. The focus of this chapter is how this cross-centeredness works out in the real life of a believer. First of all, we will look at some essential components of cross-centeredness. This will not be an exhaustive list, but will include some extremely important truths. Then, we will examine some practical application.

ESSENTIAL COMPONENTS OF CROSS-CENTEREDNESS

Sound Understanding of the Cross

There are so many aspects of the work of Jesus Christ—so many glories of his cross. These truths affect our lives as believers. They give us hope, bring about endurance, generate growth, produce inner strength, produce sanctification, and so much more. We must grow deeply in these truths. We must know them, meditate upon them, and preach them to ourselves constantly. Paul said in 1 Corinthians 2:2 that he "determined not to know anything among you, save Jesus

Christ, and him crucified." Does this mean that Paul only evangelized while in Corinth? Not at all. It means that he did not proclaim human philosophies like the Greek orators and teachers in that city. His focus was on the person and work of Jesus Christ. The Corinthians learned cross-truths! There was a good reason that Paul chose this style of ministry. He states it clearly in verse 5 of the same passage: "That your faith should not stand in the wisdom of men, but in the power of God." Paul understood very well that man-centered faith would not do. It would not stand the test of time. Trials and tribulations would destroy faith that was superficial and spurious, faith based on great oratory ability or human philosophy. Believers must know sound theology. We must all be good theologians by the grace of God. The Scriptures are full of Christ-centered, God-glorifying truths about the work of the cross. Pulpits ought to be sounding out cross-centered messages constantly. Believers ought to be filling their hearts and minds with gospel truths. We must be taught truths like our election, calling, justification, adoption, sanctification, and glorification. We must be learning about the work of our high priest being done now, but only on the basis of the finished work of the cross. We need to know about his preserving grace, his intercession, and his advocacy. The cross-centered life is a life of a growing and sound understanding of the cross.

Spiritual Nourishment

This goes hand and hand with sound understanding. In chapter 6, we discussed spiritual growth. My point here is to emphasize that our souls are nourished by the cross-truths we learn. These truths are life-sustaining. We do not live by bread alone but by all of God's revealed Word to us (Matthew 4:4). Sound doctrine must not simply be reduced to theological knowledge that we can show off to others. It must sink into our hearts. It must move our affections more and more Godward. Hebrews 13:9 is an important verse that we have looked at previously. It states, "Do not be carried about with various and strange doctrines. For *it is* good that the heart be established by grace, not with foods which have not profited those who have been occupied with them." The writer is saying that the believer's heart is not established by legalistic dietary laws (or anything else legalistic for that matter). It is established by grace. He is not suggesting that this just happens. The heart is established as truths about grace are absorbed. We must hear them, understand them, delight in them, and exalt God for them! So much of the contemporary church's growth strategy is centered on people's making decisions. Impulsive, self-willed, mindless, manipulated decisions do not grow people. I have seen people make commitments at altar calls that are broken very shortly after. I have seen young people come home from Christian camp meetings "on fire" for God only to fall back into their old life of sin in a very short span of time. God is no asking us for these kind of superficial and self-generated moves. He desires us to love him in such a way that we realize that we cannot do it apart from his grace! He desires that we see ourselves in our real and true weaknesses that we may rely on his grace alone. That is why the spiritual nourishment of gospel grace grows people. Out of hearts filled with Christ, right decisions will be made. Christ will be exalted in our dependence.

Affliction

Now here is an element of cross-centeredness that tends to be foreign to believers in western culture. But this must not be ignored. God uses affliction in our lives for very important reasons. He shows us his sovereignty and strength. He reveals to us our great and many weaknesses. He brings us to the realization that we are completely dependent upon him. He draws us close to himself so that we see our great need to look upward. In 2 Corinthians 1:9, Paul testifies concerning his own afflictions, "Yes, we had the sentence of death in ourselves, that we should not trust in ourselves but in God who raises the dead." God was using Paul's miseries and suffering to bring Paul to new levels of trust in himself. Peter teaches that Christ's suffering was an example for us to follow and that we should rejoice when we bear reproach for the faith for it brings glory to God (1 Peter 2:21; 4:13–14). Any affliction that comes our way ought to be committed to the glory of God. This is an important reality of the Christian faith. We must not wither and fall away when suffering and hardship comes our way. We must understand that God is sovereign and good and perfect. In suffering, he is not letting us down! He is drawing us close. Do you believe that God's grace is sufficient? Will you be content in whatever circumstances that God brings you to (Philippians 4:11–13)? Affliction is part of cross-centeredness. We understand that our Savior suffered an infinite, incomprehensible suffering on our behalf. We understand that our light afflictions are God working for us that we might be conformed to Christ's image (2 Corinthians 4:17).

Ownership

Cross-centeredness means that believers understand that through the cross our lives belong to God in a special way. "Or do you not know that your body is the temple of the Holy Spirit *who is* in you, whom you have from God, and you are not your own? For you were bought at a price; therefore glorify God in your body and in your spirit, which are God's" (1 Corinthians 6:19, 20). In salvation, God has set us apart for himself. There is a Biblical sense of our being sanctified already. This is not the sanctification of condition, because we are certainly not perfectly holy! It is the sanctification of status (We briefly mentioned this before).We have been set apart to God in Christ. It means we belong to God. We now seek his will and kingdom. We are his bondslaves. This does not mean that we serve unwillingly. No! Service has been transformed into a joy. Listen to Paul's words in the face of impending persecution as he planned to go to Jerusalem. "But none of these things move me; nor do I count my life dear to myself, so that I may finish my race with joy, and the ministry which I received from the Lord Jesus, to testify to the gospel of the grace of God" (Acts 20: 24). His desire was to joyfully finish his ministry. The idea of belonging now to God, means that life is now about him. Body and soul, we are his. Understand that, because of our new disposition in regeneration, and because of the Holy Spirit's indwelling, belonging to God delights us! God is our Master, but he is also our Father. We love him. It is all because he first loved us (1 John 4:19).

Now that we have explored some of the essential components of cross-centeredness, we will examine some application. How does the cross affect our daily lives? How do some of the above truths make a difference on a daily basis? What does cross-centeredness look like?

PRACTICAL APPLICATION OF CROSS-CENTEREDNESS

Humility

The gospel humbles the human heart. We have already seen that one of the most significant truths in the Scriptures is that we do not deserve to be saved. There is truly no place for boasting except in the cross of Jesus Christ (1 Corinthians 1:29, 31; Galatians 6:14). As a believer studies the doctrines of the gospel, he must be struck by the degree of his depravity more and more. I have many times presented to lost people the fact of their sinfulness. Most often, however, there is no understanding of what that means, never mind the depth of their depravity. It must not be so among believers. It should not be "Yes, I am a sinner, but so what? Everyone sins." I had been a believer for many years before I came to understand God's grace in a deeper way. I recognized that I, in no way, contributed to my salvation. I repented. I believed. I came to Christ—but it was all of grace. God had to draw me (John 6:44). God had to change my heart (Ephesians 2:4–5). Apart from his work, I would still be continuing in my rebellion. Believers must see in the cross the measure of their sin. There is no such thing as a *little* sinner. All humans are guilty big time! We are rebels void of any spiritual sensibility. Romans 8:7–8 put it this way: "Because the carnal mind *is* enmity against God; for it is not subject to the law of God, nor indeed can be. So then, those who are in the flesh cannot please God." It is clear that all are spiritually dead before the quickening work of the Spirit of God begins in a human heart. Jesus purchased my salvation on the cross. His atonement brought about even my faith in him. As I see these doctrines in Scripture, what does it do? It humbles me. The cross-centered life is a humble one. But for the grace of God, I would be lost forever. Before salvation, I walked in the lusts of my flesh. I was a child of disobedience (Ephesians 2:2–3). These truths do not depress me. They do not dampen my human spirit. I do not flog myself each night because of my natural depravity. Why? I flee to the cross! I realize that, because of the grace of God, I am a new creation. I have known his grace. I have tasted his goodness and it is exceedingly good. These truths do not depress me, but they do humble me!

Dependence

This goes hand in hand with humility. *God is glorified in our dependence upon him.* The fact is that God has specifically ordained redemption so that redeemed human beings glory in him alone. Salvation is not really *God's part* and *our part*. It is all God's part. Does that mean that we do not do anything? No. Philippians 2:12–13 surely show both sides. These verses state, "Therefore, my beloved, as you have always obeyed, not as in my presence only, but now much more in my absence, work out your own salvation with fear and trembling; for it is God who works in you both to will and to do for *his* good pleasure." So, there is a sense in which we have a part. We repent, we believe, we pray, we do works, we cooperate with the Spirit of God. So why do I say that it is all of God? It is because we could not do our part unless God did his part. In fact, God's doing of his part assures that we will do ours. In other words, our part flows out of God's sovereign grace. If not, there would be room for our boasting and there is no room for our boasting in salvation! His saving grace is 100 percent effective. Even our faith is a gift (Ephesians 2:8–9). This is extremely important. We must take no credit for our salvation. We must not see it even as 99.9 percent God and 0.1 percent us. If I were to ask you as a Christian, what the difference is between you and someone who is an unbeliever, I hope your response would ultimately be that the difference lies with God and not yourself. This truth about our salvation is the foundation for my point that God is glorified in our dependence. 1 Corinthians 1:29–31 is a remarkable passage that teaches the above truths. It tells us that no one can boast in the presence of God. It is of God in Christ that we have righteousness and sanctification. There is only boasting in the Lord. To him alone belongs the glory. He is the source of all the good that we as redeemed people have. He is "our wisdom and our righteousness and sanctification and redemption." Thus, in a very real and significant way, believers are entirely dependent upon God. Further, notice in the above verses that this dependency is so that there is no boasting except in him. I often say from the pulpit, "It is not that believers should not boast. We can and should boast a great deal. But all of our boasting ought to be about God not us!"

The more we see Jesus Christ as our all-sufficiency, the more we will take proper notice to give him glory as we depend on his enabling grace. One of the great truths I have come to see in Scripture over the last several years is the dynamic working of grace. It is seen clearly in 2 Corinthians 12:8–10. Here, the apostle Paul relates the account of his asking for his "thorn in the flesh" to be removed. I take this to be a reference to some major physical affliction of Paul's. In any event, whatever this problem was, Paul asked three times for its removal. He got an answer to his prayer. Christ said, "My grace is sufficient for you, for My strength is made perfect in weakness" (verse 9). Notice that "strength" is used in concert with "grace." In other words, Christ's grace here meant his strength! The point is that God's grace is dynamic (active) not static. He keeps on giving it. It is an enabling grace. This passage brings forth the truth that it is a sufficient grace. In verse 9, it is also equated with Christ's power! In Christ we have all we need. Paul recognized what Christ was saying to him. No wonder he exclaimed, "Therefore I take pleasure in infirmities, in reproaches, in needs, in persecutions, in distresses, for Christ's sake. For when I am weak, then I am strong" (verse 10). I believe that Paul thought that this was a better answer than if the Lord told him that he would remove his infirmity! In trials, it is extremely important that believers recognize his sufficient grace. When we recognize his grace and our dependency upon it, when we actually are dependent upon it, Christ is glorified. It is then that we are acknowledging his infinite greatness and worth. We are recognizing in a real way that apart from him we can do nothing (John 15:5). This is what makes *self-performance* Christianity so wrong. It is dependence on self. It therefore glorifies self. This is what makes *payback* Christianity so wrong as well.

By *payback* Christianity, I mean a manner of living in which the Christian thinks he is paying back God for that saving grace God bestowed upon him at conversion. One cannot payback grace! It would then cease to be grace (a giving of unmerited, undeserved favor). Instead of thinking that after conversion, we live to pay God back, we must understand that our need is for more grace to be poured out upon us. We need more grace, and that is exactly what we get! We must live lives that are grace-driven. So God is glorified in our dependence upon him.

Worship

Of course, the above humbling and dependence leads to real worship of God. How can we not praise and worship the God who brought such a salvation to us. In the cross, we see most clearly his love, goodness, greatness, wisdom, and power. Because of our new spiritual eyes, we behold his beauty, holiness, glory, and majesty. We understand that he is God. There is no other God. There is no one like him (Isaiah 46:9). He is worthy of all of our honor and glory. Perhaps it is appropriate here to look at some verses that express God's worthiness of worship.

Psalm 8:9 O LORD, our Lord, How excellent is Your name in all the earth!

Psalm 63:1–3 O God, You are my God; Early will I seek You; My soul thirsts for You; My flesh longs for You In a dry and thirsty land Where there is no water. So I have looked for You in the sanctuary, To see Your power and Your glory. Because Your lovingkindness is better than life, My lips shall praise You.

Psalm 104:1 Bless the LORD, O my soul! O LORD my God, You are very great: You are clothed with honor and majesty.

Psalm 92:5 O LORD, how great are Your works! Your thoughts are very deep.

Psalm 150:2 Praise him for his mighty acts; Praise him according to his excellent greatness!

Isaiah 40:28 Have you not known? Have you not heard? The everlasting God, the LORD, The Creator of the ends of the earth, Neither faints nor is weary. his understanding is unsearchable.

Ephesians 3:20–21 Now to him who is able to do exceedingly abundantly above all that we ask or think, according to the power that works in us, to him *be* glory in the church by Christ Jesus to all generations, forever and ever. Amen.

1 Timothy 1:17 Now to the King eternal, immortal, invisible, to God who alone is wise, *be* honor and glory forever and ever. Amen.

Revelation 4:11 You are worthy, O Lord, To receive glory and honor and power; For You created all things, And by Your will they exist and were created.

Revelation 5:12 Saying with a loud voice: 'Worthy is the Lamb who was slain To receive power and riches and wisdom, And strength and honor and glory and blessing!'

We look forward someday to being in his presence forever where there is fullness of joy (Psalm 16:11). We understand, all of this is because of grace alone, because of the cross. This worship isn't simply for an hour a week at church. However, it certainly ought to be there at church. It is there that we corporately make much of him. We come together to praise his name, to sing about his glory. How does cross-centeredness affect us in reality? For one thing, churches that are cross-centered ought to have real corporate worship going on. The joy ought to be visible, and the praise ought to be loudly sounded out! Then we leave our corporate worship to go into the world and live for his glory in a continual worshipful state of heart. The worship continues in our daily lives. Each day ought to be viewed as an opportunity to praise his name. Cross-centeredness means real worship.

Victorious Transformation

Here now is one last application of cross-centeredness. It transforms our lives into lives of victory. By this, I mean that hope is alive in us. We understand that Christ's death was the Father's will. He was pleased with Jesus Christ. The cross brought full atonement. How do we know that God the Father was pleased? A few times in Christ's life, the Father spoke of his being pleased audibly. He did this at Christ's baptism and transfiguration (Matthew 3:17; 17:5). The Father did not do so at the cross. Instead, he verified that he was pleased and gave us assurance that Christ made atonement for sin by doing something very special. He raised Christ from the dead (Romans 1:3; 4:25)! Now, because Jesus lives, we live in the fullness of his resurrection. Believers have victory in Jesus (1 Corinthians 15:57). As we abide in him, he makes us fruitful. His character is formed in us by the Holy Spirit (Galatians 5:22–23). His grace is sufficient. When we are weak, we see his strength in us (2 Corinthians 12:9–10). Literally, we are his new creation (2 Corinthians 5:17; Ephesians 2:10). This fruitful life is to be seen by others in order to bring him glory. Jesus told us so himself when he said, "Let your light so shine before men, that they may see your good works and glorify your Father in heaven" (Matthew 5:16). May others see this transformation in our lives. May we point them directly to the cross. Peter encourages Christians to show forth the excellencies of our God. "But you *are* a chosen generation, a royal priesthood, a holy nation, his own special people, that you may proclaim the praises of him who called you out of darkness into his marvelous light" (2 Peter 2:9). The word *praises* in this verse means *virtues*. Believers are to be showing forth God's excellent greatness by the victorious transformation that has taken place in their lives. A life lived for the glory of God must be cross-centered. This focus is sure to keep us on the right track. We must not take our eyes away from the gospel of Jesus Christ. It must be central. In the next chapter, I want to point out something that we must not do with the gospel. We must not treat it as an add-on to our lives.

10

The Problem of the Gospel as an Add-On

T HE GOSPEL must never be something that we treat frivolously. If we are going to live lives that actively glorify God, we must not move from the actual good news concerning Jesus Christ's person and work. Sadly, this has happened in our postmodern culture. There is a shallowness in the way the gospel is presented in many churches. I don't say this carelessly. I have given it much thought over many years. I have seen this shallowness firsthand. I was once a participant. Some years ago in his powerful book *The Gospel According to Jesus,* John MacArthur addressed contemporary gospel shallowness directly. He writes in the first chapter about warnings not to take the gospel lightly: "Present-day evangelicalism, by and large, ignores these warnings. The prevailing view of what constitutes saving faith continues to grow broader and more shallow, while the portrayal of Christ in preaching and witnessing grows fuzzy."[1] MacArthur goes on in the book to rebuke a gospel call that ignores repentance, genuine faith, and true discipleship. This book was first published in 1988. Since then, I believe, many people have echoed MacArthur's concerns. Many have been concerned about getting the gospel right.

1. MacArthur, *The Gospel According to Jesus,* 21.

Some have addressed the problem of man-centeredness in gospel presentations. Is it important to deal in this book with these shallow, man-centered problems concerning how the church proclaims the gospel? Does this truly relate to glorifying God? I believe that it does. If the gospel is simply an add-on to one's life, it will not transform. That is because the gospel cannot simply be attached to that which already exists. It ceases to be the gospel when it is preached as an attachment. Many people talk about being "saved" as if it were simply some external rite that was performed as they said some words about Jesus. They performed the rite and then were pronounced "saved" by the one "evangelizing" them. What great problems have been created by those who have devised and performed manipulative evangelistic methods to *manufacture* converts! In this chapter, I would like to explore briefly the dangers of a "gospel" whereby Jesus is simply attached to that which already exists in one's life. This is not meant to be merely analysis. This is meant to cause those reading to think about their own salvation. Not necessarily to doubt it. That is really not my point. It is to cause the reader to think about the direction in which his own spiritual life is going. Genuine believers can live sometimes as if the gospel has been attached to one's life. The real goal is *transformation* not added benefits to the old life. Here are three areas to think about.

ATTACHMENT OR REPENTANCE

When one attaches the gospel, there is no change of mind or heart. One simply adds Christ (or at least they add on the event of their supposed conversion) to what they already are and do. But repentance, a change of mind or heart, is accompanied by a changed life. Otherwise the repentance is not real. Paul speaks of this change happening to the Thessalonian church noting that they "turned to God from idols to serve the living and true God" (1 Thessalonians 1:9). They had become servants of Jesus Christ. This is the same transformation that happened to Paul himself. Paul was acutely aware of who he was before his salvation. "And I thank Christ Jesus our Lord who has enabled me, because he counted me faithful, putting *me* into the ministry, although I was formerly a blasphemer, a persecutor, and an insolent man" (1 Timothy 1:12–13). The Thessalonians turned to Christ; Paul turned to Christ. There was a turning, a willingness to leave the old life and have a new one in Christ. There was recognition that the old life was bad at its core. The Thessalonians did not simply attach Christ to there list of pagan deities. Paul did not simply attach Christ to his Pharisaical Judaism. There was repentance. The gospel call is to repent and believe (Acts 20:21). With no call to repentance, a drug dealer might think that he can add on Christ to his life and maybe Jesus will help him be a more successful drug dealer! A successful but unscrupulous business man might think that by saying a prayer he gains heaven and can continue in his life just as it was before. The real problem is that someone might think that they can add on Christ to their self-glorying lifestyle without the need to change anything that really affects that lifestyle. They can be on their way to heaven and see nothing really wrong with self-exaltation. This is no different than if the Thessalonians added on Christ and continued to worship many pagan deities as well. I don't think Paul would have been commending them. Instead, they turned from their idols. Paul comments, "For this reason we also thank God without ceasing, because when you received the word of God which you heard from us, you welcomed *it* not *as* the word of men, but as it is in truth, the word of God, which also effectively works in you who believe" (1 Thessalonians 2:13). Paul is actually thanking them for heeding his exhortation to "walk worthy of God, who calls you into his own kingdom and glory" (1 Thessalonians 2:12). We must not attach Christ to what we already are and do. We must turn to Christ from what we already are and do, and let him transform us from the inside out. We must understand that this whole process, including repentance, is by his grace. Repentance is not someone reforming their own lives. It is not cleaning up one's life in preparation to receive Christ. It is a true turning to God through Jesus Christ by the grace and mercy of God. He grants repentance; it is a gift (2 Timothy 2:25). God touches one's heart so that they desire to be saved from not only the penalty of sin but from its power. Ultimately, they desire to be reconciled to God himself. It is nonsense to think of the gospel without repentance. Adding on Jesus to what we already are and do is foolishness.

ATTACHMENT OR GENUINE FAITH

The gospel cannot in reality be an attachment or add on. This is because the gospel calls for a response of faith. Salvation is not simply going through a ceremony that makes one saved. It is not a ritual or a rite. It is not walking down an aisle, making a profession, saying a prayer, filling out a card, making a decision, or being pronounced "saved" by someone else. The gospel calls for one to put genuine faith in a person, the person of Jesus Christ. There are aspects of this belief that characterize it as life-changing. Here are just a few of the many aspects of a faith that is genuine. Saving (genuine) faith embraces the promises of God that are in the gospel. The believer is fully persuaded that what God promises, he will perform (Romans 4:20–21). This faith contains knowledge of the facts of the gospel (Acts 2:36). It also agrees with this knowledge. There is a belief of the truths of the gospel from the heart (Acts 8:37). Genuine faith also contains the element of trust. One places all his hope and trust in Jesus Christ (2 Corinthians 1:9–10). This genuine faith is manifested by obedience to the gospel, to Christ, and from one's heart (Romans 6:17). Certainly, we are not speaking of perfect obedience in any way. We remain quite imperfect until we reach glory with Christ. Lastly, the Scriptures teach that this genuine faith is a lifelong continuous faith, not a one-time event (Hebrews 10:38–39). All these elements of genuine faith contradict the idea that the gospel can simply be attached to one's life without any real subsequent internal and even external change. Many times a Christian will doubt his salvation because he cannot pinpoint some specific conversion event when he accepted Christ. The real question to be asked however is if one possesses real faith. It is real faith that saves—and real faith continues throughout one's life. One may not remember when he came to this faith. The important thing is that one ought to be able to know if he really believes. Is he living the life of real faith in Jesus Christ? This is the crucial question. Every believer must also realize that this genuine faith is also a gift of God. "For by grace you have been saved through faith, and that not of yourselves; *it is* the gift of God, not of works, lest anyone should boast" (Ephesians 2:8–9). Once again, salvation is all of grace so that God alone is glorified!

ATTACHMENT OR DISCIPLESHIP

The third reason to be on your guard toward an add-on gospel (which I hope I have already conveyed is clearly a false gospel) is that an add-on gospel removes the call to discipleship. Christ's call is a call to follow him. There is no such thing as having two masters. Jesus made this clear enough in the Sermon on the Mount. "No one can serve two masters; for either he will hate the one and love the other, or else he will be loyal to the one and despise the other" (Matthew 6:24). He calls us to believe him as our Lord and Master. This is not to say that, from the beginning, we have this all together. But as we grow, it becomes more and more clear that we are to break completely away from the world and be completely consecrated to him. Attaching the gospel to one's life is not exactly the same as taking up one's cross daily and following Christ (Luke 9:23). We cannot separate conversion from a call to discipleship. Remember, glorifying God actively is our chief aim. How can this mean anything less than acknowledging that he is the sovereign Lord of the universe? Can I believe that he is the sovereign Lord of the universe except over me? How unreasonable! Coming to Christ means coming to my Lord and Savior. It means I recognize that I am called to follow him. I am called to actively live for his glory.

WHAT DIRECTION ARE YOU GOING?

As we examine our spiritual lives (which we are called on to do—see Romans 12:3; 2 Corinthians 13:5), we must think directionally. Attaching the gospel to what we already are and do, leaves us pretty much the same in our being and actions. Christ becomes a nice thing to have in one's life. You know—a life with good old-fashion values: family, faith, being a good neighbor, having friends, getting exercise, being productive. But this is not Christianity. Christianity is about glorifying God, magnifying his name, displaying his glory, proclaiming his greatness and grace. It is a radical transformation. There is a break with self-glory and an exaltation of God. Take away the gospel call to repentance, genuine faith, and true discipleship and one may well be left with something quite un-radical. There is no active living for the glory of God with a gospel simply attached to the old self.

11

God Is Pleased with What He Does

IN THIS closing chapter, I desire to, as they say these days, flesh out what a life lived actively for God's glory looks like. Of course, I have already said many things about this. Now, I am going to look in some detail at three major aspects of glorifying God. Before looking at them specifically, I want to point out the major idea: God is pleased with what he does! When this present age is done, we will see that very clearly. Allow me to begin this discussion with a quote from Jonathan Edwards' sermon titled *God Glorified in Man's Dependence*. "The glorious excellencies and beauty of God will be what will for ever entertain the minds of the saints, and the love of God will be their everlasting feast. The redeemed will indeed enjoy other things; they will enjoy the angels, and will enjoy one another; but that which they shall enjoy in the angels, or each other, or in any thing else whatsoever that will yield them delight and happiness, will be what shall be seen of God in them."[1] Notice Edward's implication that all we enjoy in eternity will ultimately be recognized as God's work. From the very beginning we see God pleased with that which he made. For it says in Genesis 1:31, "Then God saw everything that he had made,

1. Edwards, "God Glorified in Man's Dependence," 41, 42.

and indeed *it was* very good . . ." When the Bible tells us that mankind was made in God's image, the point is that human beings were designed to reflect God's glory. In the salvation process, God ultimately redeems man so that he once again can truly reflect God's glory. My point is that being made in the image of God glorifies God not man. We point to him. In salvation, we are remade by him, again to reflect his glory. Ephesians 2:10 says that "we are his workmanship." Paul makes a similar point when he writes, "For who makes you differ *from another*? And what do you have that you did not receive? Now if you did indeed receive *it,* why do you boast as if you had not received *it?*" (1 Corinthians 4:7). How can we boast about that which was not intrinsically ours but has been given to us by God? We cannot and we must not. With these things in mind, let's now examine three main areas in which we can actively glorify God.

HUMBLE SERVICE

This is an area fraught with possible misunderstanding. Remember our five huge truths. One of them was that God has no needs. In that section we quoted Acts 17:25 which says, "Nor is he worshiped with men's hands, as though he needed anything, since he gives to all life, breath, and all things." We said that there is a sense in which human beings do not and cannot serve God! There is nothing we can actually do for him. Yet, there is another sense in which we are called to serve our Lord and Savior. That is exactly why this point is fraught with misunderstanding. If we do not distinguish between the kind of service we are called to and that which we are certainly not called to, we will not glorify God at all. In his book *God's Greater Glory*, theologian Bruce Ware describes the difference between the concept of serving over God and serving under God.[2] Ware's point is quite clear and convicting. It is the *serving under God* that is proper for us to do. The idea of *serving over God* is dishonoring to our sovereign, omnipotent God. Let me see if I can express the differences here briefly. Many believers have the idea that they are helping God out. God really needs our help. He has left a lot of things up to us. If we will only answer his call, then his purposes will truly be accomplished. If we do not serve, then his purposes will be terribly frustrated. They think, "Poor God, he really is desperate for our assistance. Well, lucky for him, some of us have answered the call. We will do the job." How many times is our Christian service framed in language that makes us the heroes! This is serving over God. The concept is horribly wrong. Though it may not be exactly expressed as I have described, it is a real problem and a real abomination to God. No one will frustrate his purposes! He is God. He will accomplish his good pleasure (Isaiah 46:10).

The kind of service that glorifies God is the "serving under God" kind. This is when we understand God's graciousness in allowing us to be means through which he shows his glory. We are simply vessels of clay through which he displays his power. We understand it is all by God's grace. We understand that the whole time we are doing whatever it is that we are doing, we have not merited on our own anything by what we did. This is the whole idea of Jesus' parable in Luke 17:7–10. He closes this parable with these words: "So likewise you, when you have done

2. Ware, *God's Greater Glory*, 195–203.

all those things which you are commanded, say, We are unprofitable servants. We have done what was our duty to do" (v.10). The idea here is that we always operate on the grace side of things not the merit side. We could never pay Christ back for our salvation. We do not even try. We still need more grace. Service is a privilege. Service is still his work in us. It is clear that this serving glorifies God because it pleases him (Colossians 1:10). Here again, we must be careful. Remember, God is pleased with his work. So our service must be his work, accomplished in his power, using his gifts, and for his glory alone.

GOOD WORKS

This is closely related to the humble service discussed above. While we might think of the humble service above as more formal ministry, these good works should be happening all the time. Jesus clearly states the principle as follows: "Let your light so shine before men, that they may see your good works and glorify your Father in heaven" (Matthew 5:16). The question we must answer is, "how can a believer's good works glorify God if they are the believer's good works?" Thus, it important for us to explore the relationship between a believer's good works and God's glory. Let's begin with the fact that one's doing of good works is not automatically God-glorifying. The danger is that good works may in their essence possess a deadness in their relationship to God's glory (Hebrews 9:14). They may be done without genuine faith, joy, or love (Hebrews 11:6; Acts 20:24; 1 Corinthians 13:3). They certainly may be done for self-glory (Philippians 2:3; Galatians 6:26). Ignoring one's heart while doing some good deeds is a grave mistake. God is not honored by joy-less, faithless, loveless service.

Works that do glorify God are a fruit of one's salva-tion and testify of it (Romans 2:6–10; Ephesians 2:8–10). Good works are performed by God's grace from the gifts and abilities that he gives us (1 Corinthians 15:10; Galatians 2:20; 1 Peter 4:11). Thus, these works please God because they are ultimately his work in us (Philippians 2:13). Once again, remember the underlying truth that God is pleased with what he does! One more thing is important to see here. We must distinguish between obeying Christ by do-ing good works and loving Christ. In John 14:15 Jesus said, "If you love Me, keep My commandments." The *keep* in this verse can be understood to be in the indicative mood rather than the imperative. Thus, Christ is saying that if one loves him, one will keep his commandments. Thus, loving Christ and the obeying Christ are inextricably linked together. However, at the same time, they are to be distinguished. Loving Christ is not obeying him. Obeying Christ is not loving him. Obeying Christ is the product of loving him not the actual loving. The distinction is important. One might simply do good things and think that the doing itself is sufficient. However, the Scriptures indicate that the loving comes first. Remember what Jesus asked Peter in John 21. Three times he asked Peter if Peter loved him. Each time he asked, Peter affirmed his love for Christ. After Peter re-sponded each time, then Christ commanded Peter to feed his sheep. The primary question is love. That is why we must cultivate our love for Christ. We must desire to know his love deeply (Ephesians 3:18–19)! Out of a heart of love, comes a life of glorifying God!

GENUINE FRUIT

If it seems like these three points all run together, it is because they do. They are all the external result of what God is doing in our soul! One of these works is genuine fruit. Fruit is the figure of speech used in Scripture to picture the outward, visible influence of the Spirit of God in our hearts. Thus the New Testament speaks of the fruit of the Spirit (Galatians 5:22–23). Jesus also used the picture of a vine and its branches (John 15). Christ is the vine; true believers are the branches. As we abide or remain in him, his life flows through us. It is his life in us that produces fruit. An unfruitful branch is actually evidence that Christ's life is not present. Thus Jesus said in John 15:5, "Without Me you can do nothing." This verse speaks unmistakably about our complete dependence on Jesus Christ. He has ordained his followers to go forth and bear fruit. In John 15:8 he said, "By this My Father is glorified, that you bear much fruit; so you will be My disciples." This fruit encompasses all that is produced from God's work in us. It includes others we have a part in bringing to Christ, those we encourage in the faith, and those who see our good works and glorify the Father. This fruit is seen in our praises and worship. It is seen in the nine fruit of the Spirit listed in Galatians 5:22–23. It is seen in so many other ways. It is the visible product of God working in and through us! It glorifies God because it is actually his work.

GOD'S GLORY IS OUR DELIGHT

As we looked at these last three points, I hope it is clear that God is pleased with his own work. As we have sought to understand better in this book what it means to live actively for the glory of God, I hope the importance of this subject has been driven home. There is, of course, so much more than this simple writing. I would like to leave you with this final thought. God, who has no needs, created us so that we might know him and enjoy him. This is not arrogant of God. It is because he is absolutely glorious that his creating us is very gracious and loving. Someday we will be in his presence. What we see and know by faith now will be sight. Let me close with the words of John Owen from *The Glory Of Christ*: "While we are still on earth, faith, beholding the glory of Christ, will give us a foretaste of future glory. There is no glory, no peace, no joy, no satisfaction to be found in this world compared to what we get from the weak and imperfect view which we have of the glory of Christ by faith. Thus while we are still in the world, faith gives us such a foretaste of future blessedness in the enjoyment of Christ as may continually stir us up to say with the psalmist, 'I shall be satisfied when I awake in your likeness.'"[3] May this foretaste of glory Divine stir you up to live actively for the glory of God alone!

3. Owen, *The Glory of Christ*, 126.

Bibliography

Edwards, Jonathan. "God Glorified in Man's Dependence." In *Jonathan Edwards On Knowing Christ*. Edinburgh: Banner of Truth Trust, 1990.

———. "The Justice of God in the Damnation of Sinners." In *Jonathan Edwards On Knowing Christ*. Edinburgh: Banner of Truth Trust, 1990.

Ferguson, Sinclair B. *Grow in Grace*. Edinburgh: Banner of Truth Trust, 1989.

Horton, Michael. *Christless Christianity*. Grand Rapids, Michigan: Baker, 2008.

Lloyd-Jones, Martin. *The Cross*. Wheaton, Illinois: Crossway, 1986.

MacArthur, John, Jr. *The Gospel According to Jesus*. Grand Rapids, Michigan: Zondervan, 1988.

Owen, John. *The Glory of Christ*, abridged by R. J. K. Law. Edinburgh: Banner of Truth Trust, 1994

Piper, John. *God Is the Gospel*. Wheaton, Illinois: Crossway, 2005.

———. *Pierced by the Word*. Sisters, Oregon: Multnomah, 2003.

Schreiner, Thomas R., and Ardel B. Caneday. *The Race Set Before Us*. Downers Grove, Illinois: InterVarsity, 2001.

Ware, Bruce. *God's Greater Glory*. Wheaton, Illinois: Crossway, 2004.

Wells, David. *The Courage to be Protestant*. Grand Rapids, Michigan: Erdmans, 2008.

Made in the USA
Columbia, SC
03 September 2018